alex mcfarla

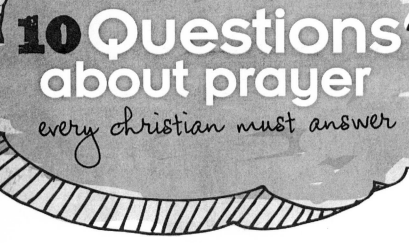

10 Questions about prayer
every christian must answer

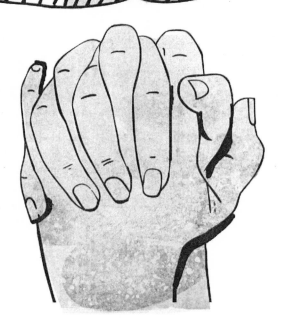

ACADEMIC

NASHVILLE, TENNESSEE

B&H Publishing Group
Nashville, Tennessee

ISBN: 978-1-4336-8217-9

Dewey Decimal Classification: 248.3
Subject Heading: PRAYER \ CHRISTIAN LIFE \ SPIRITUAL
LIFE

Printed in the United States of America

Contents

Preface

What Is Prayer?

Before we talk about prayer, we must define it and tell how it should be used. Why? Because non-Christians often think of prayer in a completely different way than Christians do. We must compare apples with apples. Sometimes non-Christians criticize prayer, but they do not have a proper understanding of Christian prayer. It is important to be on the same page so we talk *to* each other instead of *at* each other.

Prayer is talking to God based on a relationship with God. Prayer is communication with God. But prayer is more intimate than talking to a friend. Prayer is a family relationship. It is like talking to your father. That is the way Jesus described it.

> Whenever you pray, you must not be like the hypocrites, because they love to pray standing in the synagogues and on the street corners to be seen by people. I assure you: They've got their reward! But when you pray, go into your private room, shut your door, and pray to your Father who is in secret. And your Father who sees in secret will reward you. When you pray, don't babble like the idolaters, since they imagine they'll be heard for their many words. Don't be like them, because your Father knows the things you need before you ask Him. (Matt 6:5–8)

Since prayer is a family relationship, you must know the heavenly Father to pray to Him. And Jesus is the only way to the Father. "I am the way, the truth, and the life," Jesus said. "No one comes to the Father except through Me" (John 14:6). In other words, Jesus says there is no other means of access to God. The Creator of the universe graciously grants people to have a relationship with Him through His Son Jesus Christ.

The Bible has many things to say about this relationship to the Father. Jesus said, "Unless someone is born again, he cannot see the kingdom of God" (John 3:3). To experience physical birth is not enough; a person must have a second birth into God's family—a spiritual birth. Jesus said the Father gave "the right to be children of God" to those who "receive" Jesus and "believe" in Him (John 1:12). Though all people stand before God as condemned sinners (Rom 3:23), God sent His Son to take away the sin of the world (John 1:29). Jesus sacrificed Himself as a perfect substitute for sinners (2 Cor 5:21) so that they might be saved. Those who trust in Jesus receive eternal life (John 3:16) and are adopted as God's children (Gal 4:4–5). As a child of God, you can talk (pray) to Him, making requests of God the Father through Jesus Christ (John 14:13).

Having defined prayer in this way, it is easier to see why so many individuals have difficulty with the notion of prayer. Nonbelieving critics may have difficulty with prayer because they fail to understand the nature of a Christian's relationship to God in prayer. Even believers may have difficulty with prayer if they misunderstand the basis for prayer in a relationship with God. Perhaps the voice of the critic has caused the believer to question some of the fundamental biblical truths about Christian prayer. It is for these reasons that we have written this book.

The purpose of this book, then, is not devotional, seeking to move you to prayer. Of course, we hope you will be motivated to pray as you find answers to those pressing questions about the nature of prayer. Nor is this a practical handbook on prayer offering you instructions on how to pray, though we believe you will receive encouraging tips on prayer. Finally, this book does not describe the various ways to pray, although you will be challenged to consider alternative forms of prayer.[1] Fundamentally, this book is an apologetic approach to prayer. The questions we have selected serve as the antithesis of this book; they are the problems we seek to answer.

The Approach and Plan of *10 Questions*

This book addresses ten questions commonly asked about prayer. Some are more likely to be raised by non-Christians or even by those opposed to Christianity. Yet even serious Christians have questions about prayer. Identifying those questions and uncovering the motives behind them will put us in a better position to answer them.

In cases where questions about prayer are levied by non-Christians as a means of casting doubt on fundamental biblical truths about the Christian faith, the book will use an apologetic approach. *Apologetics* refers to a reasoned defense of Christianity. The word *apologetics* comes from the Greek word *apologia*, which means "a defense." The related verb *apologeomai* ("to defend oneself") is used in Acts when Paul gives his trial defense before Festus and Agrippa (Acts 26:1–2). Peter tells believers to be ready to defend their faith: "But honor the Messiah as Lord in your hearts. Always be ready to give a *defense* to anyone who asks you for a reason for the hope that is in you" (1 Pet 3:15). Apologetics exists to remove intellectual barriers to Christianity by answering questions raised by skeptics and nonbelievers. Christians who use apologetics present a rational basis for the Christian faith by defending it against objections, misrepresentations, and attacks.

Therefore, in this book we will use apologetics to defend the Christian practice of prayer by appealing to logic and common understanding. Once we establish the rationality of prayer, we will then seek to answer a given question on the basis of biblical precepts and practices.

The plan of this book will entail a counterpoint/point structure. Each chapter will assess opposing viewpoints to the question at hand in the "Counterpoint" section. We will then follow the "Counterpoint" with a "Point" section outlining the perspective of the authors. The "Point" section will offer several "Prayer Principles" defending our position based on firm biblical, theological, and philosophical principles.

Endnote

1. To see a complete listing of the various ways to pray and the principles to follow when praying, see Elmer Towns, *The Prayer Journey Bible* (Shippensburg, PA: Destiny Image Publishing, 2011). The appendix lists 549 different ways to pray, pp. 1965–2111.

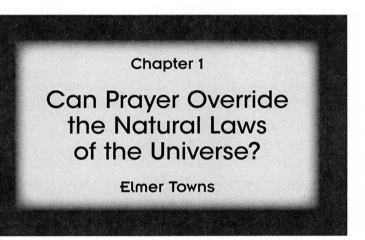

Chapter 1

Can Prayer Override the Natural Laws of the Universe?

Elmer Towns

How powerful is prayer? James 5:16 teaches that the prayer of a righteous person is powerful and effective. What example did James give as evidence for this claim? He cited the prophet Elijah, a man whose prayers held back rain for more than three years in the land of Israel. The same God who created the heavens and the earth (Gen 1:1) also held the power to control whether rain fell from the sky upon the land.

While the Bible includes many examples of God's intervention in the laws of nature, there is much debate regarding whether He continues to operate in this way today. Should we pray for God to intervene to change the course of nature in order to answer our prayers? The answer to this question has vast implications, ranging from how we pray regarding natural disasters to how we intercede on behalf of loved ones with sickness or disease. In this chapter we will first look at the argument of those who would answer this question negatively. Second, we will respond with a few Prayer

Principles that seek to account for the biblical evidence. Third, we will conclude with several observations applicable to our own lives as we seek to both understand and live a life of prayer that reflects an accurate interpretation of Scripture. As we do, we hope you will find yourself strengthened and encouraged not only by the stories of God at work throughout history but also by how He can change lives—including yours—today.

Counterpoint

Not everyone believes God overrides the natural laws of the universe to answer prayer. Among them are three categories of individuals. First, there are those who deny the existence of God at all. Those who hold to this view are called atheists. While the number of people in our society who hold to atheism is a small minority, it includes a vocal and growing number of Americans. For example, best-selling author and atheist Sam Harris wrote concerning Hurricane Katrina:

> What was God doing while Katrina laid waste to their city? Surely He heard the prayers of those elderly men and women who fled the rising waters for the safety of their attics, only to be slowly drowned there. These were people of faith. These were good men and women who had prayed throughout their lives. Do you have the courage to admit the obvious? These poor people died talking to an imaginary friend.[1]

The outspoken atheist Dr. Richard Dawkins referred to another writer on this issue stating, "He noted that every Sunday, in churches throughout Britain, entire congregations prayed publicly for the health of the royal family. Shouldn't they, therefore, be unusually fit, compared with the rest of us?"[2] Since the royal family is not "unusually fit" compared with the rest of society, Hawkins argues that prayer has no impact on the lives of people.

Another category of individuals are those who remain uncertain of whether God exists. Those who hold to this view are called agnostics. The views of agnostics have some affinities with atheists but are in general much less committed to a particular view of God. A rising group of individuals in this category labeled the "Nones" now comprise approximately 19 percent of all Americans.[3] Now more than ever our society faces a time when many people either oppose the idea of God's intervening within natural laws to answer prayer (atheists) or are uncertain if this is even possible (agnostics).

In addition, historically another category of individuals argues that God does not interfere with natural law. Popular during America's early history, Deism teaches that a divine Creator God set the universe in motion, yet does not intervene in daily life. Founding fathers such as Benjamin Franklin and Thomas Jefferson are often listed among those who held to this view.

There are many other perspectives on divine intervention in addition to the three briefly mentioned above. Islam, for example, argues for a god who intervenes according to the teachings of the Qur'an, while eastern religions such as Buddhism and Hinduism emphasize the view that God is in all things. In what follows, we will seek to determine what the Bible teaches on this important question. In so doing, we will discover that God has not only intervened over natural law in the past; He also declares He can continue to do so today.

Point

Logically, those who believe in an all-powerful God must at the very least accept that God *could* intervene in the laws of nature to accomplish His will. As one writer notes,

We can safely conclude that within the Christian perspective of God, he possesses attributes that allow him to access laws of the universe that we do not know about and use them, in combination with his divine power in nature, to bring about the miraculous. There is nothing illogical about this. Therefore, there's nothing illogical about God performing miracles.[4]

However, our concern is whether God *has* intervened in the past as well as whether He *can and does* continue to intervene today. Since the Scriptures will serve as our primary source of evidence, it is important first to consider how it portrays God's intervening in the laws of nature in the form of miracles.

In the New Testament the following four Greek words are primarily used to refer to miracles:

1. *Semeion*—a "sign", i.e., an evidence of a divine commission; an attestation of a divine message (Matt 12:38–39; 16:1, 4; Mark 8:11; Luke 11:16; 23:8; John 2:11, 18, 23; Acts 6:8, etc.); a token of the presence and working of God; the seal of a higher power.
2. *Terata*—"wonders;" wonder-causing events; portents; producing astonishment in the beholder (Acts 2:19).
3. *Dunameis*—"might works;" works of superhuman power (Acts 2:22; Rom 15:19; 2 Thess 2:9); of a new and higher power.
4. *Erga*—"works;" the works of Him who is "wonderful in working" (John 5:20, 36).[5]

In each case a miracle was a sign or working of power that performed something that defied human explanation. How has God supernaturally intervened? Numerous examples could be provided, but here are seven occasions that clearly reveal God suspended the known laws of the universe to accomplish a miracle:

- Jesus and Peter walking on water
- Jesus raising the dead (Jairus's daughter, the widow's son, and Lazarus)

- God sending fire and brimstone on Sodom and Gomorrah
- God raining bread daily from heaven (the manna in the wilderness)
- Jesus feeding 5,000 with five loaves of bread and two small fish
- Jesus giving sight to a blind man
- Jesus turning water into wine

None of these seven miracles could be adequately explained apart from an intervention in the normal working laws of the universe. The only other option is to conclude that the miracles have been inaccurately recorded in Scripture, which would call into question the integrity of the Bible. It is beyond the scope of this book to offer a full treatment of the evidence for the Bible's inspiration and authority. Other scholarly works have shown that Scripture has been faithfully preserved and accepted from the earliest times as being from God, and the Bible itself attests to its own divine origins (2 Tim 3:16–17; 2 Pet 1:20–21). We will, however, offer a few governing Prayer Principles to help explain why God can intervene in the laws of nature and how this truth relates to prayer.

Prayer Principle: God, the Creator of all things, can create a higher law, suspend existing natural laws, or work within existing laws to answer prayers as He chooses.

God can answer a prayer with a higher law than the existing natural law. Notice how the law of gravity is overridden in a human-made, antigravity chamber where people float and turn somersaults in the air. If machines can supersede the law of gravity, so can God.

If we believe there is a God who has created all things, then the largest miracle has already taken place, namely creation. Other miracles or divine interventions in the universe are therefore certainly within His power. According to C. S. Lewis, a miracle is "an interference with Nature by supernatural power."[6] God answers prayer to do the miraculous for His purposes, not ours. So when we pray, we ask according to God's will (Matt 6:9) and according to His Word (John 15:7). Yet we also desire for God to answer according to His divine purpose.

Prayer Principle: Biblical prayer assumes and expects the miraculous.

I personally believe in miracles because the Bible declares miracles will happen. In addition, I have seen God do the miraculous in answer to prayer, both in my life and in the lives of others. The Christian philosopher argues for God's existence by stating that if there are laws, there must also be an ultimate Lawmaker. But could we not also suggest that if there is an ultimate Lawmaker, then He could interrupt His laws for His purpose?

While it is one thing to conclude from the biblical evidence that God has intervened in the past, it is quite another to say that He still intervenes in the present. There are those who maintain that the time of miracles has passed. Is this true? While we might not experience the same types of miracles seen by the prophets or apostles of Scripture, there is no biblical reason to conclude that God does not continue to work in miraculous ways to accomplish His purposes today. We will look at the various types of miracles noted in Scripture to better understand how God has worked throughout history and can work today in response to our prayers.

First, there are one-time miracles. In creation God brought together matter, energy, time, space, laws, and life. This miracle of creation was a one-time event that will not be repeated today. There are also other miracles listed in the Bible that were one-time events such as the virgin birth of Jesus, His resurrection, and His ascension to heaven.

Second, there are sign miracles. These sign miracles serve as powerful demonstrations of God's power recorded in Scripture. The purpose of sign miracles is to show God's power and glory. These involved Jesus calming the storm on the Sea of Galilee and the many miracles Jesus did in healing the sick of various diseases and infirmities.

When you think of a sign miracle, think of the signs you see in your travels. Signs are constructed to give you direction, information, or to confirm what you know. In the same way, God gave a sign of direction to Moses through a burning bush (Exod 3:1–9). There were also some signs warning of danger, such as the ten plagues in Egypt where miracles were used to warn Pharaoh and the Egyptians. Some signs make announcements. For example, the angels appeared to the shepherds in the field in order to announce the birth of Jesus Christ (Luke 2:8–20). Other signs give confirmation of a divine call or commissioning. Gideon prayed for the wool of a lamb to be wet and the ground dry. God confirmed His call to Gideon through this sign miracle (Judg 6:36–40).

Third, there are power-demonstrating miracles. People expected the Messiah to have great power. When Jesus Christ stopped the winds and waves, people observed that "even the winds and the sea obey him" (Matt 8:27). In that miracle He demonstrated He could do what only God does. He demonstrated that He was God. According to the Gospels, Jesus performed at least thirty-seven specific miracles. John 21:25 further adds, "And there are also many other things that Jesus did, which, if they were written one by one, I suppose not even the world itself could contain the books that would be written."

In the Old Testament, God used certain people to perform power-demonstrating miracles as well. The Lord provided two such miracles during the time He spoke to Moses at the burning bush. Moses was to use these miracles in the presence of Pharaoh. (Exodus 4). The parting of the Red Sea offered yet another powerful sign that God was at work in Moses and had provided an escape or "exodus" for His people out of Egypt. Further signs were provided through Moses during the forty years in the wilderness to reveal God at work in his life and in the life of the community of the Israelites.

The ministry of Elijah provides another biblical example of God's using a power-demonstrating miracle to reveal His work through His servants and to draw people closer to Him. The most significant of the sign miracles performed in the life of Elijah involved his calling down fire from the sky to prove that the Lord was the one true God (1 Kgs 18:38–39). In response the people turned from worship of Baal and honored the Lord.

Fourth, there are providential miracles. The word *providence* comes from the Latin *providere*, which means, "to foresee." In His foreknowledge God sees what is going to happen, then brings all things together to occur according to His will. I like to explain providence similar to the role of the director of a film. First, the director must see the end product in his or her mind. Then the he or she must direct the scenes of the film to accomplish this vision. This includes the instructions given to the actors, the editing work in postproduction, and even how the film is marketed to its audience. The director may never appear on camera, yet his or her work is evident in every frame of the movie. Similarly, God may not always show up as the star actor but may sometimes arrange circumstances in such a way as to accomplish everything according to His divine will.

Therefore, God answers our prayer with providence. God can work behind the scenes to arrange the proper conditions to answer our requests when we pray. John D. Morris explains providential miracles in this way:

> Consider *miracles of providence.* These occur when God acts *within* His ordained natural processes to bestow His benevolence on His creation. They may involve the precise timing of a natural occurrence, or an unusual rate of a process. A providential event may be extremely unlikely from a statistical point of view, but within the realm of possibility. Usually we consider miracles to be something

desirable, a gift of God's grace, but they may be quite catastrophic—a judgment or a chastisement.

Miracles could affect either believers or unbelievers. For believers, God answers prayers, fulfills promises, provides every need, corrects wrong behavior, and in general, shows His favor. To unbelievers, He can likewise show His favor, or punish wrongdoing. He demonstrates to all that He exists and exhibits His desire that all be saved.[7]

Even in our actions, then, the Lord directs our steps and guides our movements to accomplish His purpose. The end result is sometimes a miracle; yet God need not always interfere with the laws of nature. Instead, God can work providentially through natural laws. God rules the world by His laws and can certainly use the powers of the laws already in place to accomplish His will.

Fifth, there are miracles of conversion. When Jesus said, "You must be born again" (John 3:7), He explained that when a person becomes a follower of Jesus Christ, he or she receives new life. Miracles can lead to a conversion as an unbeliever is convicted of sin and future judgment (John 16:7–11). When the Holy Spirit convicts us of sin, our spiritual blindness is removed so we see our sin as it really is. When we have a full understanding of our lost condition before God, we are motivated to cry out for salvation. This process is nothing short of miraculous.

The Holy Spirit then causes us to understand the gospel by removing the blindness of unbelief. Paul spoke of this in 2 Cor 4:3–4: "But if our gospel is veiled, it is veiled to those who are perishing. In their case, the god of this age has blinded the minds of the unbelievers so they cannot see the light of the gospel of the glory of Christ, who is the image of God." When people testify of their conversion they often say, "It took a miracle for Christ to save me."

In fact, the miracle of conversion was of tremendous importance in the start of the early church. On the day of Pentecost, more than 3,000 people came to faith in Jesus and were baptized that day (Acts 2:41). The book of Acts records three other additional conversion accounts as well, often including other miraculous events in the immediate context:

- The conversion of many Samaritans (Acts 8:5–25): In this account, the early Jewish believers were surprised at the conversion of non-Jews to the faith.
- The Ethiopian eunuch (Acts 8:26–39): One of the top leaders in Ethiopia happened to be reading the prophet Isaiah when Philip was led to share the gospel with him. The man believed and was baptized immediately, with Philip miraculously disappearing afterwards.
- The Philippian jailer (Acts 16:25–33): An earthquake opened the doors of the prison, leaving the jailor considering suicide at the thought of the prisoners under his command escaping. Instead, Paul and Silas stopped him, shared the gospel, and led the man and his family members to faith in Jesus late that night.

The apostle Paul's conversion is one of the most dramatic accounts in Scripture of a miraculous conversion. On the road to Damascus to arrest Christians, he was blinded by a bright light and experienced a vision of Jesus. Paul remained blind for three days until a believer named Ananias, who likewise experienced a vision from Christ, restored Paul's sight. Paul was baptized and became the leading missionary to the Gentiles in the early church. Both the conversion and the circumstances surrounding his conversion were supernatural.

Later, Paul would write,

I received mercy because I acted out of ignorance in unbelief. And the grace of our Lord overflowed, along with the faith and love that are in Christ Jesus. This saying is trustworthy and deserving of full acceptance: "Christ Jesus came into the world to save sinners"—and I am the worst of them. But I received mercy for this reason, so that in me, the worst of them, Christ Jesus might demonstrate His extraordinary patience as an example to those who would believe in Him for eternal life. (1 Tim 1:13–16)

He viewed God's work of conversion in his life as powerful evidence of God's mercy as an example to others.

Sixth, there are miracles of God's guidance. The Holy Spirit directs or guides the believer (Gal 5:16). When the Holy Spirit leads us, we can have confidence that we are children of God: "All those led by God's Spirit are God's sons" (Rom 8:14). God comes to humans and works in our thoughts, desires, emotions, and aspirations—all to guide us into the divine purpose He has chosen.

God also leads believers through many external means that would not necessarily be considered miraculous. We often refer to these leadings as open or closed doors (1 Cor 16:9). God often leads through consulting friends (Prov 11:14) as well as collective wisdom to solve the problems of our culture (Prov 16:1).

Seventh, there is the miracle of answered prayer. The Bible indicates that Jesus promised unlimited results through prayer: "Whatever you ask in My name, I will do it so that the Father may be glorified in the Son" (John 14:13). But when you look at the conditions Jesus placed on answered prayer, we find that these promises are limited. Therefore, to understand what miracles God *does* answer in prayer, we need to look at the other teachings Jesus gave regarding His answers to our requests. Otherwise, we can claim one promise out of context and have an inaccurate understanding of prayer.

Prayer Principle: There are conditions governing God's miraculous intervention in the form of answered prayer.

Jesus offered at least six clear conditions regarding in our lives. First, Jesus taught that our prayers would be answered when we live according to God's Word. He shared, "If you remain in Me and My words remain in you, ask whatever you want and it will be done for you" (John 15:7). In 1 John 3:21–24 we also learn,

> We have confidence before God and can receive whatever we ask from Him because we keep His commands and do what is pleasing in His sight. Now this is His command: that we believe in the name of His Son Jesus Christ, and love one another as He commanded us. The one who keeps His commands remains in Him, and He in him.

Second, God also teaches that He answers prayers because we pray with confidence. First John 5:14 notes, "Now this is the confidence we have before Him: Whenever we ask anything according to His will, He hears us." This is not a call to be boastful in our prayers but rather to come to the Lord confident that He can and will answer according to His perfect will.

Third, Jesus taught that our prayers are answered because we are involved in serving Christ. Jesus said, "I appointed you that you should go out and produce fruit and that your fruit should remain, so that whatever you ask the Father in My name, He will give you" (John 15:16).

Fourth, God answers when we pray continually and consistently. Jesus clearly noted in Luke 11:9 the continuous aspect of prayer stating, "So I say to you, keep asking, and it will be given to you. Keep searching, and you will find. Keep knocking, and the door will be opened to you." We are to continue to ask, seek, and knock. This was not a call to a single time of prayer but to an ongoing lifestyle of intercession.

Fifth, we will receive answers in prayer when we ask in faith believing that we will receive an answer. Jesus taught, "Therefore I tell you, all the things you pray and ask for—believe that you have received them, and you will have them" (Mark 11:24). Our prayers are to be humble, yet also directed in confidence to the Lord, knowing that He hears and responds.

Sixth, we must make sure we turn from sin so God will hear us and answer our requests. For example, the psalmist wrote, "If I had been aware of malice in my heart, the Lord would not have listened" (Ps 66:18). That's because "we know that God doesn't listen to sinners, but if anyone is God-fearing and does His will, He listens to him" (John 9:31). This does not mean God cannot "hear" physically the prayers of every person. The idea is that He desires to answer those who are living according to His ways.

Seventh, Jesus promised that we could do even greater works than He did only through the power of the Holy Spirit. Jesus commanded, "I assure you: The one who believes in Me will also do the works that I do. And he will do even greater works than these, because I am going to the Father" (John 14:12). This verse seems to promise believers will be able to do everything Jesus has done. But does this verse mean we can calm a tropical storm, heal leprosy, or raise the dead? Notice carefully, this verse did not promise we could do the *same* works as Jesus. It said we could do *greater* works.

Why did Jesus teach His followers would have the power to perform greater works than He did? It is because He promised to send the Holy Spirit to live in and empower the lives of those who believed in Him. The Holy Spirit was the power that worked in Jesus and works in us as well. Take a look at the four ways the Holy Spirit's power was displayed through Jesus: "Jesus . . . full of the Holy Spirit" (Luke 4:1); Jesus "was led by the Spirit" (Luke 4:1); "Jesus returned . . . in the power of the Spirit" (Luke 4:14); and "The Spirit of the Lord is on Me, because He has anointed Me" (Luke 4:18). When we are empowered by the Holy Spirit as Jesus was, we can accomplish the works of God that the Holy

Spirit desires just as He did through Jesus. Yet our sinful nature and human weaknesses (Rom 7:12–20) may help explain why we often do not allow God's Spirit to work in our lives as effectively as Jesus did.

Some also suggest that the "greater works" we are able to accomplish include sharing the gospel with others and seeing them come to faith in Jesus Christ. While the healing of a person from sickness or disease provides a powerful testimony to God's ability to heal, its impact is limited to this life. When we share the gospel and someone comes to faith in Jesus, the impact is eternal (John 3:16).

Conclusion

Miracles are not spread out evenly throughout the Bible. During the lifetime of Moses, God performed numerous miracles to bring His people out of Egypt and provide for the Israelites in the wilderness for forty years. During the ministries of the prophets Elijah and Elisha, numerous miracles were also recorded that revealed God's power at work through them. The earthly ministry of Jesus and His earliest followers was likewise marked with a significant number of miraculous acts. Yet between these periods of time, far fewer miracles were recorded in Scripture.

For example, in the New Testament John the Baptist was not listed as a miracle worker. We are instead told, "John never did a sign, but everything John said about this man [Jesus] was true" (John 10:41). So if you ask for a miracle and it does not happen, do not think you are less spiritual or that there is something wrong with your prayer life. Jesus said that John the Baptist was the greatest man to have ever been born of a woman (Matt 11:11); yet John did not perform miracles.

Answers to prayer can often be seen through providence when God works behind the scenes to bring about the answers we seek. On occasion God will heal supernaturally or intervene in a miraculous way. On other occasions God's answer is no because it is not His will. Sometimes God asks us to wait; He intends to answer our prayer but according to His timing rather than ours. Yet many times God hears our prayers and answers positively, providing a perfect response to fit our time of need. The exact form of His answer may differ from what we originally requested, but He answers according to His perfect will on each occasion. Often He answers, "Above and beyond all that we ask or think according to the power that works in us" (Eph 3:20). When He does, we find that whether God intervenes to alter the laws of the universe or works within them, His perfect love is revealed in ways that communicate His grace for our times of need.

S. M. Lockridge was the pastor of Calvary Baptist Church in San Diego, California, from 1953 to 1993. He is well known for a passage from his sermon titled "He's My King" that illustrates the power of Christ to do as He wills in regard to our prayers. I pray its words encourage and inspire you as we conclude this chapter:

He's enduringly strong, He's entirely sincere, He's eternally steadfast. He's immortally graceful. He's imperially powerful. He's impartially merciful. He's God's Son. He's a sinner's Savior. He's the centerpiece of civilization. He stands alone in Himself. He's unparalleled. He's unprecedented. He's supreme. He's preeminent. He's the loftiest idea in literature. He's the highest idea in philosophy. He's the fundamental truth in theology. He's the miracle of the age. He's the only One able to supply all of our needs simultaneously. He supplies strength for the weak. He's available for the tempted and the tried. He sympathizes and He saves. He guards and He guides. He heals the sick. He cleans the lepers. He forgives sinners. He discharges debtors. He delivers captives. He defends the feeble. He blesses the young. He serves the unfortunate. He regards the aged. He rewards the diligent. He beautifies the meek. Do you know Him?

Well, my King is the king of knowledge. He's the well-spring of wisdom. He's the doorway of deliverance, He's the pathway of peace. He's the roadway of righteousness. He's the highway of holiness He's the gateway of glory, He's the master of the mighty. He's the captain of the conquerors. He's the head of the heroes. He's the leader of the legislators. He's the overseer of the overcomers. He's the governor of governors. He's the prince of princes. He's the King of kings and the Lord of lords.

His life is matchless. His goodness is limitless. His mercy is everlasting. His love never changes. His word is enough. His grace is sufficient. His reign is righteous. His yoke is easy, and His burden is light.

Well, I wish I could describe Him to you. But He's indescribable. Yes, He's incomprehensible. He's invincible, He's irresistible. I'm trying to tell you, the heavens cannot contain Him, let alone a man explain Him. You can't get Him out of your mind. You can't get Him off of your hands. You can't outlive Him, and you can't live without Him. Well. The Pharisees couldn't stand Him, but they found out they couldn't stop Him. Pilate couldn't find any fault in Him. Herod couldn't kill Him. Death couldn't handle Him, and the grave couldn't hold Him. That's my King![8]

What, then, should our attitude be in prayer? The weakest believer, like a young child, can talk to the heavenly Father. The poorest sinner, like an impoverished beggar, can reach out to God in prayer. The ability to call on God is one of the attributes that distinguishes people from animals. We are spiritual beings, created in God's image to worship Him. As we pray to God, we thank Him in advance for answering our prayers, knowing He will respond according to His perfect will. We can praise Him for who He is, what He has done, and what He will do in the future.[9]

Endnotes

1. Sam Harris, *Letters to a Christian Nation* (New York: First Vintage, 2006), 52.

2. Richard Dawkins, *The God Delusion* (New York: Mariner, 2006), 63.

3. "'Nones' on the Rise," The Pew Forum on Religion and Public Life, October 9, 2012, http://www.pewforum.org/Unaffiliated/nones-on-the-rise.aspx, accessed September 16, 2013.

4. Matthew Slick, "Do the Laws of Logic Contradict Miracles?" CARM.org, http://carm.org/do-laws-logic-contradict-miracles, accessed September 16, 2013.

5. "Miracles," *Bible Encyclopedia*, http://christiananswers.net/dictionary/miracle.html, accessed September 16, 2013.

6. C. S. Lewis, *Miracles* (New York: HarperOne, 1960), 5.

7. John D. Morris, "Is It Scientifically Possible for Miracles to Occur?" Institute for Creation Research, http://www.icr.org/article/1164, accessed September 16, 2013.

8. The popular video of this sermon is available as of September 16, 2013 at http://www.youtube.com/watch?v=ynGNIGpjE7o.

9. Elmer Towns, *Bible Answers for Almost All Your Questions* (Nashville, TN: Thomas Nelson, 2003), 219.

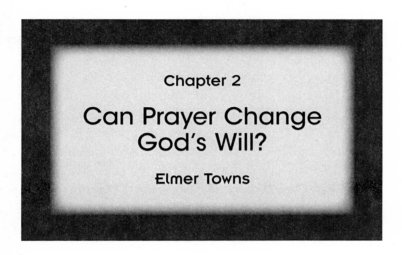

Chapter 2

Can Prayer Change God's Will?

Elmer Towns

When we look at the pages of the Bible, it appears that God already has a perfect plan in place; yet He also calls us to pray to Him regarding our requests and to seek His will. The tension between these two truths inevitably leads to the question that will occupy us in this chapter: "Can prayer change God's will?" If we can accomplish more than God's predetermined plan with our prayers, what does that say about God and the permanence of His will? In this chapter we will first look at some of the various ways this issue has been challenged by critics. Second, we will respond with a more biblical view which seeks to hold these two truths in tension. Third, we will provide a few important Prayer Principles to guide us toward a more helpful perspective on prayer which allows for a God who works in the lives of believers but also maintains His perfect will that has existed since before the foundation of the world.

Counterpoint

If God is all-powerful and has a predetermined plan for the universe, how can our prayers change His plans? In the spectrum of responses to this question, two extremes stand out. On the one hand are those who overemphasize the sovereignty of God and on the other are those who overemphasize human free will. Regarding the former, some critics reject the claim that prayer can change the will of God. Those who hold this view appeal to biblical texts such as Mal 3:6 which says, "I, Yahweh, have not changed." Such texts have important implications for evangelism. When we pray to ask God to save a lost person, for example, those who hold this view would deny that such prayers are effective if God has not already chosen or "predestined" that person for salvation.

On the other side of the spectrum are those who overemphasize human free will. Although representing only one category of thought in this camp, an increasingly popular trend is open theism. Open theism maintains that God can "change His mind" based on how people on earth pray or live. Just as Abraham seemed to "negotiate" with God in Genesis 18, or Moses pleaded for God's mercy on the people of Israel after God planned to judge them, open theism suggests believers can change God's future plans through their intercessions. For example, outspoken advocate Greg Boyd suggests, "Much of it [the future], open theists will concede, is settled ahead of time, either by God's predestining will or by existing earthly causes, but it is not exhaustively settled ahead of time. To whatever degree the future is yet open to be decided by free agents, it is unsettled."[1]

Point

The presuppositions of both of these spectrums—(1) those who emphasize God's sovereignty at the expense of human free will, and (2) those who emphasize human free will at the expense of God's sovereignty—are damaging and contrary to other clear teachings in Scripture. A critique follows of both perspectives followed by several Prayer Principles based on the conviction that a correct perspective lies somewhere between the two views.

First, this view regarding those who emphasize God's sovereignty at the expense of human free will emphasizes only God's sovereignty without considering God's commands to pray to Him regarding our needs and requests. For example, even Jesus taught in the Lord's Prayer to ask for our daily bread (Matt 6:11). Jesus also commanded His followers to make disciples of all nations (Matt 28:18–20), though Scripture is clear that not everyone will come to faith in Him. James taught that the prayer of a righteous person is powerful and effective (Jas 5:16), and 1 Timothy 2 teaches that believers should pray for the salvation of all people, including governing leaders.

In addition, such a view implies that intercessory prayer is of little or no importance since God has already predetermined His will for the universe. Why, then, did Jesus teach His followers to pray? Why did Jesus Himself offer numerous examples of prayer in His own life? Why did the earliest followers of Jesus emphasize prayer as critical to personal holiness and to the life of the early church (Acts 2:42)? An unhealthy overemphasis on God's sovereignty can often diminish the importance of intercessory prayer, evangelism, and the pursuit of holy living. Since believers are clearly commanded to pray for others, share the gospel, and live holy lives, this view remains inadequate and unbalanced.

Second, regarding open theists who emphasize human free will at the expense of God's sovereignty, scholar Richard L. Mayhue has evaluated Boyd's views observing several weaknesses:

1. The history of orthodox Christian doctrine declares against, not for, Boyd's position.
2. Boyd's book, *God of the Possible*, depends on philosophy, not theology, to prove its point.

3. Boyd's views deify man and humanize God.

4. Boyd discards the unknown, mysterious dimensions of God in his discussions.

5. *God of the Possible* is built on an aberrant methodology.

6. *God of the Possible* fails to account for literary devices such as anthropopathism (ascribing human emotions and feelings to God).

7. Boyd's position diminishes aspects of God's deity, making God appear limited in power.

8. Boyd downplays determinative biblical texts.[2]

Mayhue discusses each of these weaknesses and supports his assertions. He claims, "These alone dismiss *God of the Possible* as impossible for evangelicals to embrace as a true biblical representation of Almighty God."[3]

In other words, while it may appear God can and does change His mind in response to our pleas, Scripture is clear God's nature and purposes do not change. He responds to and acts on our prayers; yet these responses fall within His divine foreknowledge of all things, potential and possible, that could occur. The view of open theism fails to reflect the overall message of Scripture. Though God is often presented as merciful and forgiving of those who repent, God Himself does not change in His character or nature. He is already perfect, infinite, sovereign, and has no need to change (Heb 1:10).

In fact, a variety of Scripture passages affirm God's perfect knowledge of all people and things—past, present, and future:

- God knows the hearts of all people: "The heart is more deceitful than anything else, and incurable—who can understand it? I, Yahweh, examine the mind, I test the heart to give to each according to his way, according to what his actions deserve" (Jer 17:9–10).

- God knows the motives of all people: "For Jesus knew from the beginning those who would not believe and the one who would betray Him" (John 6:64).
- God knows the thoughts of all persons: "But He knew their thoughts and told the man with the paralyzed hand, 'Get up and stand here.' So he got up and stood there" (Luke 6:8).
- God knows the past and the future: "Remember what happened long ago, for I am God, and there is no other; I am God, and no one is like Me. I declare the end from the beginning, and from long ago what is not yet done, saying: My plan will take place, and I will do all My will" (Isa 46:9–10; also Isa 48:3–5).
- God knows all things and is unlimited in power: "He counts the number of the stars; He gives names to all of them. Our Lord is great, vast in power; His understanding is infinite" (Ps 147:4–5).
- God cannot add to His already perfect knowledge: "Who has directed the Spirit of the LORD, or who gave Him His counsel? Who did He consult with? Who gave Him understanding and taught Him the paths of justice? Who taught Him knowledge and showed Him the way of understanding?" (Isa 40:13–14).

Open theism may appear reasonable upon initial consideration; yet a close look at Scripture affirms the view of God's unchanging nature rather than presenting God as uncertain about future events and open to change based on the pleas of His created beings.

Instead of accepting a view of God that either overemphasizes God's sovereignty to the point that intercessory prayer has little value or a view that teaches God changes in response to our prayers, the biblical view is that *God is powerful enough to create a plan for each person in the universe, yet incorporate each person's free will and prayers into His perfect plan.* The following five Prayer Principles offer evidence to support this perspective.

Prayer Principle: God's eternal, perfect plan flawlessly blends with God's purposes at work in our prayers.

God is truth (John 14:6) and His Word is truth (John 17:17). God does not contradict Himself, nor does He speak contradictory statements. However, God is infinite (unlimited), and our minds are finite (limited). While we cannot fully comprehend how God's sovereignty and our prayers fit together, God is able to exercise His perfect plan for each person and at the same time allow each individual to control his or her own destiny in terms of freedom of choice, including how we pray.

How can this be true? Humans think based on finite laws; yet God operates at a level beyond our understanding. In His nature God blends two apparently opposing forces. Scripture maintains that He works out everything according to His plan. Ephesians 1:11, for example, states that God works all things "according to the purpose of the One who works out everything in agreement with the decision of His will." Likewise, Rom 8:28 says, "All things work together for the good of those who love God."

Both free choice and God's predetermined choices are taught in Scripture. God holds them together even if we cannot. Isaiah 55:9 states, "For as heaven is higher than earth, so My ways are higher than your ways, and My thoughts than your thoughts." Our inability to fully comprehend God's ways is a reflection of the fact that "the hidden things belong to the LORD our God, but the revealed things belong to us and our children forever, so that we may follow all the words of this law" (Deut 29:29). God reveals what we need to know, not everything we would like to know.

The Bible illustrates this truth in Gen 38:1–11. Scripture presents Joseph as a spoiled teenager who bragged to his brothers and parents about the special things God would do in His life.

God revealed information to Joseph in a dream, but his special knowledge turned his brothers against him. They plotted murder but instead sold Joseph into slavery. His brothers acted in sin; yet God allowed their sin to save the people of God and many others. Looking back, Joseph told his brothers, "You planned evil against me; God planned it for good to bring about the present result—the survival of many people" (Gen 50:20). Even the evil actions of people fall within God's sovereign plan. Within this narrative we find Joseph relying on God and finding his purpose in life.

Prayer Principle: Time does not limit God as it limits humans.

Since God created time, He exists outside of it and beyond it. He can see the end from the beginning and knows the final page of history before it begins. He plans and performs at the same instant. There is no yesterday, today, or tomorrow with God (Rev 1:4, 8, 11). God stands beyond time and looks down on all the choices we make. While we certainly make choices, God plans for our choices and sees them before they happen. As the apostle Paul wrote, "It is God who is working in you, enabling you both to desire and to work out His good purpose" (Phil 2:13).

When we pray for a person to come to faith in Christ, God places that desire in our hearts. When we ask God to heal a loved one from sickness, He is already at work to accomplish His perfect will in the situation. Yet the Bible also clearly speaks regarding our human responsibility. If we don't pray for our family's salvation, we may be "accountable for their blood" (Ezek 33:6). If we do not honestly face our problems or the obstacle blocking progress in our lives and ministries, the failure remains our responsibility (2 Cor 5:11, 14). We should plan and pray as though everything depends on us, but we exercise faith in God to do supernatural works so that His will goes forward.

Prayer Principle: The Bible offers a proper understanding of the plan of God.

The following is a chronological list of the order by which God decreed the events of this world.

- God decided to create a massive universe—including our world—that was good and beautiful. This world was created to operate by natural laws as an extension of His nature and as the forces by which He would rule the world. His universe would reflect the uniformity and regularity of His laws. He decided that the world would be reproducible and all living and growing life would have its "seed . . . in itself" (Gen 1:12 KJV) for reproduction.

- God decided to create people in His image (Gen 1:27). He predetermined that humans would have His nature and serve as the crowning act of His creation. And so, God gave humans freedom and autonomy.

- God decided to give humans freedom to obey or reject His plan and laws for the universe. This freedom of choice was focused in the command, "You are free to eat from any tree of the garden, but you must not eat from the tree of the knowledge of good and evil, for on the day you eat from it, you will certainly die" (Gen 2:16–17). Humanity could choose to live in harmony and fellowship with God in the cool of each day. When humans worshipped and lived in community with God, the Lord was magnified, reflecting the purpose of His creation.

- God warned against disobedience. The Lord promised immediate consequences of death, "The day you eat from it, you will certainly die" (Gen 2:17). Soon Adam and Eve rebelled against God's command, "The woman . . . ate it; she also gave some to her husband, who was with her, and he ate it" (Gen 3:6). Yet they did not immediately die because we later read, "Adam's life lasted 930 years; then

he died" (Gen 5:5). What happened? Adam died spiritually the day he disobeyed God, but he lived physically for
930 years.

• God decided humanity would suffer the consequences of
their sin and rebellion. When the woman sinned, God
said to her, "I will intensify your labor pains; you will bear
children in anguish. Your desire will be for your husband,
yet he will rule over you" (Gen 3:16). God's punishment of
the man was,

> Because you listened to your wife's voice
> and ate from the tree about which I com-
> manded you, "Do not eat from it": The
> ground is cursed because of you. You will
> eat from it by means of painful labor all
> the days of your life. . . . You will eat bread
> by the sweat of your brow until you return
> to the ground, since you were taken from
> it. For you are dust, and you will return to
> dust. (Gen 3:17, 19)

• God decided to provide a perfect Savior for all people.
The Savior had to come from outside of the world since it
was the only way to save those within the world who had
rebelled against God. In Gen 3:15, we find this promise
to Eve: "I will put hostility between you and the woman,
and between your seed and her seed. He will strike your
head, and you will strike his heel." The seed of the woman
would be a son who would bruise the head of the serpent
(Satan). Even though God informed Adam and Eve in the
garden of His plan to save them, God had an eternal plan:

> For you know that you were redeemed
> from your empty way of life inherited from
> the fathers, not with perishable things like

silver or gold, but with the precious blood of Christ, like that of a lamb without defect or blemish. He was chosen before the foundation of the world. (1 Pet 1:18–20)

The death and resurrection of Jesus Christ was God's plan throughout eternity.

- God's plan reveals that all who believe and claim salvation in Jesus Christ can be saved. In addition, God also determined that all those who will not believe in His Son will live separated from God in eternal punishment. Though not all will believe, God's desire is for all to trust in His Son and have everlasting life (John 1:29; 3:16, 36).

God's decree encompasses the entire spectrum of human history—from the creation of the universe to the new heavens and the new earth (Revelation 21–22). In the end God is the focus of redemptive history as expressed through the creation, fall, and restoration of those who trust in Him through His only Son, Jesus.

Prayer Principle: God created us with the freedom to choose.

The fact that God allowed sin to enter the world reveals that God did not create us as preprogrammed robots. Instead, He created us as individuals, desiring that we worship and live for Him. The fact that God allowed His created beings to have freedom to rebel against Him reveals that He did not develop a totalitarian plan where free expression would be eliminated.

Prayer Principle: God created us in His image.

Because God is a free autonomous being, He created humans in His image with a free, autonomous nature. Genesis 1:26–27 clearly states,

"Let Us make man in Our image, according to Our likeness. They will rule the fish of the sea, the birds of the sky, the livestock, all the earth, and the creatures that crawl on the earth." So God created man in His own image; He created him in the image of God; He created them male and female.

Because God is a person with intellect, emotion, and will, we are likewise composed with intellect, emotion, and will. We have the power of intellect, or rational power. We can think. We have the power of emotions. We can feel love and anger, just like God. We have the power of choice. These characteristics make up personality, which expresses itself through self-perception and self-direction.

Conclusion

We have seen that God both hears our prayers and responds to them in perfect accord with His divine nature and will. We cannot accept either the conclusion that God has a predetermined plan that does not leave room for our intercessions or the view that we can change God's eternal plan through our human abilities. Instead, we see that the Lord is bigger than either option, offering a relationship with each of us that includes interaction with us through prayer. This process fits in perfect agreement with the sovereign plan He has established from before the beginning of time.

One way to look at this reality is to consider the view of philosopher Martin Buber who suggested God created humans as independent agents. Buber called this an "I-Thou" relationship.[4] God and humans are separate from each other yet joined in relationship. I call it *independent dependency*. We are *independent*, meaning we are self-governing persons. Yet God placed us in a world operated by laws of many types. These laws are an extension of God's nature and are His way to direct us. These laws make us *dependent* on God. We are both independent and dependent.

When believers know that God has a perfect will for them, they should seek to know it and strive to do it. Paul prayed for the

Colossian believers, "We are asking that you may be filled with the knowledge of His will" (Col 1:9). That means the will of God is something believers must search to know and do. As Jesus said, "If anyone wants to do His will, he will understand" (John 7:17). We conclude with a few practical observations to help you navigate the tension between God's sovereignty and human free will. The Lord's Prayer teaches us to ask, "Your will be done" (Matt 6:10). We do not ask God to change His will or to bless our will. Instead, we ask God to help us discover and live His will in our lives. When we pray, "Your will be done," we make a conscious decision to let Christ direct our lives. This includes four aspects:[5]

First, praying "Your will be done" asks God to help us find His will. Before we can do God's will, we need to know God's will. To pray "Your will be done" is a commitment to knowing God's will as it is revealed in His Word. If we long to know how God wants us to live and even how to pray, we must become students of His book. We are to "be diligent to present [ourselves] approved to God, [workers] who [don't] need to be ashamed, correctly teaching the word of truth" (2 Tim 2:15).

Second, praying "Your will be done" asks God to help us submit to His will. It is not enough just to know the will of God; we must pray it and obey it. "Your will be done" is a plea for submission. Pastor John Hamby notes that according to Rom 12:2, it is our privilege to submit to "that good and acceptable and perfect will of God" (NKJV). The truth is that the cause of all the unrest, frustration, unhappiness, and sense of powerlessness in the life of a Christian can be traced to trying to follow our own self-will. At the back of all our failure is the desire to have our own way rather than His way.[6]

Third, when we pray, "Your will be done," we are also submitting our attitude to God. Some people actually attempt to do God's will but do so with an ungodly attitude. They attend church, give financially, or serve others, but wish they were doing something else instead. When we pray for God's will to be done in our lives, we must surrender our desires to His. We actively submit to His plan with joyful anticipation of how He will work in our lives.

Fourth, praying "Your will be done" asks God to help us accomplish His will. Paul prayed for the Colossian Christians to "walk worthy of the Lord, fully pleasing to Him, bearing fruit in every good work and growing in the knowledge of God" (Col 1:10). We pray to discover God's will, ultimately desiring to see it accomplished in our lives. Our goal must not only be prayer and worship but obedience to the revealed will of God: "Does the LORD take pleasure in burnt offerings and sacrifices as much as in obeying the LORD? Look: to obey is better than sacrifice, to pay attention is better than the fat of rams" (1 Sam 15:22). Jesus also made clear, "If you love Me, you will keep My commands" (John 14:15).

Endnotes

1. Gregory A. Boyd, *God of the Possible* (Grand Rapids, MI: Baker Books, 2001), 15.

2. Richard L. Mayhue, "The Impossibility of *God of the Possible*," *The Master's Seminary Journal* 12, no. 2 (2001): 207–20.

3. Ibid., 207.

4. Martin Buber's *I and Thou*, *Angelfire*, http://www.angelfire.com /md2/timewarp/buber.html, accessed November 27, 2012.

5. Elmer Towns, *Praying the Lord's Prayer for Spiritual Breakthrough* (Ventura, CA: Regal Books, 1997), 28.

6. John Hamby, "Thy Will Be Done," Sermon Central, http://www. sermoncentral.com/sermons/thy-will-be-done-john-hamby-sermon-on -prayer-how-to-33993.asp, accessed February 2001.

Chapter 3

Is God Fair to Answer the Prayers of Some People and Not Others?

Elmer Towns

My wife grew up attending church in Saint Louis, Missouri. During World War II the women in her congregation regularly prayed for the safety of their soldiers fighting in the war. According to the testimony of those women, not one of their sons was killed even though some endured concentration camps and terrible battles. In contrast, the little town of Bedford, Virginia, had a higher ratio of young men killed during the D-Day invasion of Normandy than any other town in the United States. Of its 3,000 residents, the community lost nineteen soldiers in this battle.

Did God care more about the people of my wife's church in Saint Louis than He did for those in the town of Bedford, Virginia? Was the difference due to the prayers of these women, and, if so, did God give more favor to one group of people because their prayers were longer or more articulate? What about verses such as Acts 10:34 which state that "God doesn't show favoritism"?

In this chapter we will consider what the Bible teaches about the fairness of God in answering prayer. We will first assess several imbalanced views on the topic before examining several Prayer Principles in hopes of demonstrating that God's response is always perfect, even if it appears unfair from our human perspective.

Counterpoint

When considering the fairness of God in prayer, we must first acknowledge two extreme positions. On the one extreme are those who believe God is indiscriminate in answering prayers. All prayers, from all people, from all religions are equal. On the other extreme are those who believe that God does favor the prayers of one person over another. Those who believe God is indiscriminate in answering prayers would argue that, if there is a God, then all people pray to the same God. Consequently, those who pray in the name of any deity, Allah for example, have just as much right to have their prayers answered as Christians. According to this view, if people live conscientiously according to the standards of their religion, just as Christians live according to the standards of the Bible, then God should answer their prayers.

Important for this position is the level of sincerity and dedication among those who pray. Devout Muslims, for example, zealously pray three times a day on a mat, facing Mecca. Tibetan monks live in isolation taking vows of poverty and simplicity. Individuals from other religions commonly pray and meditate for hours each day. In many ways such dedication often exceeds that of the average Christian. From a human perspective, then, it seems that comparable dedication in prayer, regardless of religion, should have some correlation to God's answering of a person's prayer.

On the other end of the spectrum are those who maintain that God does favor the prayers of one person over another. One would expect the person who lives a more holy life to pray more powerful prayers than those who do not. The Christian who "walks in faith" should expect to live in God's favor, free from sickness and blessed in health and financial prosperity.

This is often the message, whether intended or not, given by many celebrity preachers in today's culture. The idea that those who pray more earnestly, give more generously, or perform some specific spiritual duty are more likely to have their prayers answered fits the cultural appetite of our time. In a world where we are taught that we can make our own way and that the results depend on our efforts, it's easy to give in to the temptation that our efforts make our prayers "more worthy" to be answered. Yet as we will see, God does not show favoritism, nor can our human efforts make us any more deserving of God's response. The Bible is clear that all have sinned and fall short of God's glory (Rom 3:23) and that there is no action we can take that makes us right with God apart from the grace of Jesus Christ (Eph 2:8–9).

Point

Biblically speaking, anyone who comes to God through faith in Jesus Christ can receive answers to his or her prayers. Prayer is communicating with God. Those who are God's children can talk with Him through prayer. How does God communicate with us? He primarily speaks to us through the Scriptures. Yet God has also revealed Himself through nature (Ps 19:1; Rom 1:18–20) as well as other means presented throughout the Bible, such as dreams or angelic appearances. It is important to understand how God relates to people if one is to understand better how God answers prayers. Several Prayer Principles follow, defending the position that God's response is always perfect, even if it appears unfair from our human perspective.

Prayer Principle: Prayer is based on a relationship with God through Jesus Christ.

The gospel is the basis of God's relationship with every person; therefore, the gospel is fundamental to prayer. When Adam and

Eve broke their relationship with the Lord through sin, they became separated from Him in a way only God Himself could overcome. At the proper time Jesus Christ came to earth to die in the place of sinners and suffer our punishment. John 3:16 makes clear that those who accept the forgiveness Jesus offers will have eternal life: "For God loved the world in this way: He gave His One and Only Son, so that everyone who believes in Him will not perish but have eternal life."

The Bible describes the process of receiving Jesus Christ as being born again. John 1:12–13 states, "But to all who did receive Him, He gave them the right to be children of God, to those who believe in His name, who were born, not of blood, or of the will of the flesh, or of the will of man, but of God." Jesus further states in John 3:7, "You must be born again." The word *must* points to the uniqueness of His offer. Therefore, Jesus excludes coming to the Father by any other god or method of salvation. One of the unique aspects of the Christian faith is that we can address God as "Father." The New Testament uniquely emphasizes the role of God as Father. In the Lord's Prayer, Jesus told His followers to pray, "Our Father" (Matt 6:9). God is not far off. He can be approached as an intimate Father.

Jesus personally called God "Father." In John 14:6 we find Jesus teaching, "I am the way, the truth, and the life. No one comes to the Father except through Me." We are encouraged to come before God with our needs much as a child to his or her caring parent. The term used by Jesus to refer to God in Mark 14:36 was *Abba*, a word comparable to the more affectionate English term *daddy*.

When we pray, we are like children walking into the presence of the king, our Father. The guards will not stop the boy because he is the king's child. He has immediate access to the king because they are family. When we pray to our Father in heaven, we acknowledge that we belong to His family and enjoy direct access to the King of kings and Lord of lords. This sense of intimacy provides a oneness unique to the relationship between God and His children and sets the context for how we are to understand His answers to our prayers.

Prayer Principle: God's purposes in prayer are based on divine perspective.

When we think God is not fair, it is often because we view our circumstances with only a limited human perspective. Focusing only on what we can see has many disadvantages. For example, our human perspective is often inaccurate even when we think it is right. God says, "My thoughts are not your thoughts, and your ways are not My ways" (Isa 55:8). For unbelievers, spiritual blindness limits the ability to understand God's ways: "The god of this age has blinded the minds of the unbelievers so they cannot see the light of the gospel of the glory of Christ" (2 Cor 4:4).

God did not hide Himself from those He created. God searched for Adam and Eve in the garden, a symbolic picture of God's pursuit of people throughout the ages. Jesus also illustrated this truth through the story of a shepherd who lost one of his 100 sheep. The shepherd left the ninety-nine to search for the one lost sheep. "When he has found it, he joyfully puts it on his shoulders, . . . calls his friends and neighbors together, saying to them, 'Rejoice with me, because I have found my lost sheep!'" (Luke 15:5–6). God's view of us is one that sees us as imperfect, yet created in His image and deeply loved. His response to our prayers is one way He pursues us and communicates with us in ways that are perfect from His perspective. If it appears that God answers one person's prayers and overlooks yours, it may be the result of looking at the situation from a human perspective rather than a divine perspective. He knows what we need and when we need it. God calls us to pray without ceasing (1 Thess 5:17), desires ongoing community with us, and responds with the best answer according to His perfect will.

Prayer Principle: God's answers to prayer are not detached from human emotion.

Humans were created in God's image (Gen 1:27). Therefore, the pattern and purpose of our lives comes from God. When you look into a mirror each morning to comb your hair, you see an image of yourself. When God looks at us, He sees an image of Himself, however imperfect. We too can look at God to discover many ways in which we are created in His image. For example, God is a being. More specifically, the triune God is one divine being who exists in three persons. This includes intellect, emotions, and choice. Humans have the mental capacity to think and reason, reflecting the same characteristics of our heavenly Father. Yet God knows all things actual and possible. He knows them at all times, without effort. We, on the other hand, are limited. We can increase in knowledge, but we can never know all things. We reflect God's image in terms of intellect, but His intellect stands infinitely superior to ours.

Our human emotional nature is reflected in our desires for a wide range of activities such as love, happiness, joy, peace, and our aversion for other activities such anger, distress, and sadness. These emotions likewise reflect the image of our Creator. The Bible not only teaches that God is love (1 John 4:7) but also teaches that He hates (Prov 6:16). Yet unlike humans, who often love or despise for the wrong reasons, such divine emotions find perfect expression insofar as they come from a perfect being.

We also have the power to choose, or the power of the will. We make choices based on our knowledge (intellect) and feelings (emotions). Our conscience tells us there is a God and that we should know Him (Rom 2:14–15). A reflection of our religious instinct was observed by Augustine, who said, "You have made us for yourself, and our hearts are restless until they find their rest in you."[1] Sixteen centuries later Blaise Pascal would echo, "There is a God shaped vacuum in the heart of every man which cannot be filled by any created thing, but only by God, the Creator, made known through Jesus."[2]

When we pray, our intellect, emotions, and choices are all involved in ways that allow us to express our thoughts and feelings to God. At times God answers our requests and we rejoice. At other times He answers differently or seemingly not at all, which can leave us feeling discouraged and frustrated. However, the One who made us in His image also knows how best to answer our requests. The One who gave us the ability to reason and feel emotions also perfectly understands how we feel and what we need in every moment to grow in our relationship with Him.

Prayer Principle: God is intimately aware of our needs and meets them through prayer.

One phrase in the Lord's Prayer offers profound insight regarding how God answers our needs through prayer. It is found in the sentence, "Give us this day our daily bread" (Matt 6:11). In reflecting on these words, we can discover five aspects to this Prayer Principle which will empower our prayers for God to respond to our needs.

First, we each have daily needs. While most Americans have sufficient food each day, we all have daily needs. God did not create us as self-sufficient people. We require clean air to breathe, food to eat, and water to drink. Our bodies require shelter for protection and clothing for warmth. In addition, we also require other people to provide the important social interactions that encourage us each day. These needs are met as we look beyond ourselves for help, working and connecting with others. Yet when we do, we realize we are imperfect in our attempts and stand in need of God's supernatural intervention to supply our needs.

Second, God is the One who supplies our needs. People need basic necessities such as food and water to meet their daily physical needs. We often take such things for granted; yet the Bible teaches that even these common activities have a higher purpose. Paul taught, "Therefore, whether you eat or drink, or whatever you do, do everything for God's glory" (1 Cor 10:31). Even our eating and drinking serve to honor Him. He provides food and water. For this reason prayer before meals can serve as a time of encouragement and gratitude. As we thank the Lord for what He has provided, we give Him honor and recognize Him as the Giver of all things.

Third, we must ask God to supply our needs. We often view prayer like a vending machine—we insert our money, press a button, and expect the exact item we requested at that precise moment. By using "daily bread" in the Lord's Prayer, God reveals that our needs are not supplied in this same manner. We do not speak a prayer and automatically receive each day's needs. Some suggest Christians can "name it and claim it," meaning that if we desire something, we should pray about it in faith and expect God to give us what we request. But our prayer to God must fit His will. We can "name and claim" a winning lottery number, but God will likely not honor such a prayer. Our prayers are not the persuasive words of a lawyer before a jury, pleading for what best helps our personal interests. We do not manipulate God for our every wish. Prayer is more than what you ask, more than what you do, more than what you say. Prayer is your way of living.[3]

Fourth, God supplies our needs one day at a time. The prayer, "Give us this day our daily bread" affirms the truth of God's daily provision. Just as we eat each day, we also rely on God to provide for all of our other needs on a daily and even moment-by-moment basis. Many of us live with much stress about our plans for tomorrow, the upcoming meeting at work, or an upcoming trip. Yet the phrase is often true that most of the problems we worry about never happen. Jesus offers a much better perspective for daily living. By emphasizing "this day," we ask the Lord to help us meet our needs one day at a time. Of course, there is a difference between worrying about tomorrow and planning for tomorrow. Proverbs 30:24–25 calls ants "exceedingly wise" because they plan ahead.

We can plan for tomorrow, but we are not to worry about tomorrow. God meets our needs each day as we rely on Him in prayer.

Fifth, we do not have to pray *for* everything, but we have to pray *about* everything. The Lord's Prayer does not teach us to pray, "Give us today's bread, money for the bills, a good checkup at the dentist, an oil change for the car, and a victory at tonight's game." It only commands us to pray for "daily bread." Why? "Bread" represents our essential needs. We come to God concerning our needs, but we need not list every single detail of our day. Since our Father knows what we need before we even ask (Matt 6:8), we need not worry if we forget to mention a particular prayer request. We are not required to pray for our every wish like a child who is creating a Christmas list and wants to make sure Santa has every detail. We are to ask God for our necessities but not necessarily our luxuries. The book of Proverbs offers an insightful principle in this area: "Give me neither poverty nor wealth; feed me with the food I need" (Prov 30:8).

Prayer Principle: God's fairness must be considered in light of certain conditions for answered prayer.

If the previous Prayer Principle highlights the biblical truth that God desires to provide the basic needs of all His children through prayer, this Prayer Principle holds out certain conditions for answered prayer.[4] First, you must believe that God is able. We should agree that God does hear and can answer any prayer. "Is anything impossible for the LORD?" (Gen 18:14). When we know the Word of God and believe that its promises are true, we should believe that God could do anything He promised. Beyond our biblical confidence, we also have the experience of past answers to prayer which should increase our confidence in Him.

Second, you must believe God will hear. A step beyond believing God can hear is affirming that He *will* hear. Isaiah 59:1–2 declares, "Indeed, the LORD's hand is not too short to save, and His ear is not too deaf to hear. But your iniquities have built barriers between you and your God, and your sins have made Him hide His face from you so that He does not listen."

Third, you must believe that God will answer. When we agree that God can hear and that He will hear, we are to agree that He will answer. As 1 Chronicles 5:20 observes, "He granted their request because they trusted in Him." We do not pray in doubt; we pray in faith.

Fourth, you must be yielded to God's will. When we are yielded to God, we are agreeing to His conditions. At this point the believer and the unbeliever have two different questions: The unbeliever's question is, *Can* God . . . ? The Christian's question is, *Will* God . . . ? We pray for His will and surrender to it as His humble servants.

Fifth, you must pray with urgency. Our prayers should also include a sense of urgency. When we desperately need an answer from God, we pray with fervency. As Psalm 27:7–8 shares, "Lord, hear my voice when I call; be gracious to me and answer me. My heart says this about You, 'You are to seek My face.' Lord, I will seek Your face."

Sixth, you must believe there is no other source. God answers prayer when we realize that there is no other alternative, that our back is to the wall, and that there is nowhere to turn but to God. This was the attitude of the apostle Peter when he asked, "Lord, who will we go to?" (John 6:68). He was saying that he could turn to no one but God alone. This is where weeping, begging, and fasting can serve as additional elements of our prayers.

Seventh, you must come to God with honesty and openness. We must be honest with ourselves before God. In fact, when we are also honest with other believers together in prayer, our prayers are answered.

Eighth, you should leverage the many different kinds of biblical prayer. As in all areas of life, we are to examine closely the Word of God to see all the various ways people have prayed in the

Bible. We are called to prayer in a variety of ways. First Timothy 2:1 notes, "First of all, then, I urge that petitions, prayers, intercessions, and thanksgivings be made for everyone."

Ninth, you should pray with total commitment. We must commit our lives completely to God and expect that He will answer our prayer. If we tell a friend, "I'll meet you for dinner . . . if it doesn't rain," our commitment is not sincere or dedicated. Sometimes our prayers are not sincere because we hold back. Remember God's promise: "You will seek Me and find Me when you search for Me with all your heart" (Jer 29:13).

Conclusion

Critics may claim, on the one hand, that God is indiscriminate in answering prayers or, on the other hand, that God favors the prayers of one person over another. Yet both extremes make one fatal mistake in overlooking the fact that prayer was God's idea. Consequently, God makes the rules about prayer. He knows what we need and when we need it. His desire is to work through our lives for His glory. When we come to Him by faith, we begin a relationship with Him that is ongoing, vibrant, and eternal. We can have abundant life (John 10:10) that includes our prayers to the Lord and how He answers according to His will to help us grow in Him and serve others.

While it is perhaps legitimate to ask if God is fair in answering prayers, the question ultimately remains one-sided, for it fails to see God's bigger purposes in using prayer for the benefit of others. With this in mind, we conclude with several observations regarding how our intercessions can result in significant, eternal impact in the lives of others. Scripture offers eight specific ways our prayers help others.[5] First, your prayer can save a person's life. The Bible illustrates this powerful aspect of prayer in the book of Acts. "Herod cruelly attacked some who belonged to the church, and he killed James . . . proceeded to arrest Peter too, . . . but prayer was being made earnestly to God for him" (Acts 12:1–2, 5). "The Lord had brought him out of the prison" (Acts 12:17).

Second, your prayer can move God to help someone. "Pray one for another, that ye may be healed" (Jas 5:16 KJV).

Third, your prayer can help protect others from temptation. "Simon, look out! Satan has asked to sift you like wheat. But I have prayed for you that your faith may not fail" (Luke 22:31–32).

Fourth, your prayer can help church leaders be successful in ministry. "Now I implore you, brothers, through the Lord Jesus Christ and through the love of the Spirit, to agonize together with me in your prayers to God on my behalf: that I may be rescued from the unbelievers in Judea, that my service for Jerusalem may be acceptable to the saints" (Rom 15:30–31).

Fifth, your prayer can help people understand spiritual issues. Paul prayed for the Ephesians, "I remember you in my prayers that . . . God . . . would give you a spirit of wisdom and revelation . . . that the eyes of your heart may be enlightened so you may know . . ." (Eph 1:16–18).

Sixth, your prayer can contribute to the spiritual growth of others. "I bow my knees unto the Father . . . that he would grant you . . . to be strengthened with might . . . that Christ my dwell in your hearts . . . that ye might be filled with all the fulness of God" (Eph 3:14–19 KJV).

Seventh, your prayer can influence the outcome of specific events. "Pray also for us that God may open a door to us for the message, to speak the mystery of the Messiah" (Col 4:3).

Eighth, your prayer can contribute to a peaceful society. "I urge . . . that petitions, prayers, intercession and thanksgiving be made for all people—for kings and all those in authority, that we may live peaceful and quiet lives in all godliness and holiness" (1 Tim 2:1–2 NIV).

Endnotes

1. Herbert Jacobsen, "The Precedent-Setting Revelations of Augustine's Restless Heart," *Christian History Magazine*, 15, http://www.christianhistorymagazine.org/index.php/past-pages/15augustine, accessed November 20, 2012.

2. "Blaise Pascal Quotes," *Goodreads*, http://www.goodreads.com /quotes/10567-there-is-a-god-shaped-vacuum-in-th-heart-of, accessed on November 20, 2012.

3. See Elmer Towns, *Praying the Lord's Prayer for Spiritual Breakthrough* (Ventura, CA: Regal Books, 1997).

4. Adapted from Elmer Towns, *Prayer Partners* (Ventura, CA: Regal Books, 2002), 10–13. Available online at http://digital commons.liberty.edu/cgi/viewcontent.cgi?article=1034&context= towns_books.

5. Elmer Towns, "Prayer Partners, Lesson 4," Sermon Central, http://www.sermoncentral.com/sermons/lesson-4-prayer-partners -interceding-for-others-elmer-towns-sermon-on-prayer-how-to-47528 .asp, accessed September 2000.

Chapter 4

Does God Still Answer Prayers for Supernatural Healing?

Elmer Towns

I n chapter 1 we addressed the issue of God's miraculous intervention in the laws of nature. In that chapter we responded more
directly to perspectives outside of Christianity—atheist, agnostic, and deistic. In this chapter we will more narrowly address the
question of whether God still supernaturally heals in response to
the prayers of believers. In what follows, we will focus on various
perspectives internal to Christianity.

Some believers, for example, argue that God is not the God
of disease and that every faithful Christian can live whole and
without sickness. They maintain that people with special gifts of
healing can remove sickness, disease, or even disability through
the laying on of hands or a simple prayer. Yet some so-called "faith
healers," with their often outlandish claims, have caused many
to doubt whether there are any genuine divine healings today.
Others believers maintain divine healing does not occur in our
world today. Such a view reflects a more modernist outlook that

God does not operate in today's world in the same way as in Bible times. Those who hold this view might appeal to the reality that many Christians have prayed for divine healing yet have seen their prayers remain unanswered. Instead, they would argue that God has provided medical professionals to respond to such needs, and believers should not expect miracles such as divine healing. In this chapter we will seek to provide a reasoned biblical perspective regarding prayers for supernatural healing in today's world. First, we will take a closer look at the two views mentioned above—that God always heals when we have enough faith and that God does not supernaturally heal people today. Second, we will walk through the Scriptures that reveal that God has both supernaturally healed people in the past and has the ability to do so today. In so doing, we will offer several Prayer Principles to govern the believer's approach to prayer as it relates to supernatural healing.

Counterpoint

As we will see below, the Bible portrays a God who, at times, supernaturally heals but not always. On the one hand are those who oppose the "not always" of this biblical view. They would argue that those with sufficient faith can trust God to always remove sickness from their lives. For example, the popular television minister Joseph Prince states, "God's [will] is for you to walk in abundant health and life. He does *not* want your body and life sapped, incapacitated or debilitated by pain, sickness and disease, and He will *never* withhold healing from you."[1] He then cites several passages that refer to Jesus suffering on our behalf as evidence that Jesus does not desire His children to endure sickness or pain. Many who hold this view have a distinctive doctrine of demons. They typically blame sickness and disease on demons or the Devil and suggest that a stronger faith would overpower these evil spirits and result in instant healing.

While some Christians argue that God will *always* heal those who are faithful, others reject any supernatural healing by God in our world. Those in this category could also include both atheists and agnostics who stand opposed to the supernatural, but it is perhaps just as common among Christians who interpret the Bible to teach that God does not supernaturally heal today as He did in the Bible. While the atheist or agnostic must prove there is nothing supernatural in order to disprove miracles, the Christian who rejects modern-day miraculous healings falls within a different category. He or she would accept God's ability to work supernaturally, yet deny that He does so in our world *in the same way.*

Most of those who hold to this particular view have taken a strong stand against charismatic views interpreting the Bible to teach that there are no individuals today with the gifts of miracles or healing such as presented in 1 Corinthians 12. However, the problem with this conclusion is that it assumes that if there are no people with these gifts then there are no supernatural healings or miracles. Yet God can work in a variety of ways, whether through one person, the prayers of many, or some other method that serves as part of His divine plan.

Both of these views reflect a measure of biblical truth yet remain imbalanced. If God can and does supernaturally heal people, as one extreme maintains, yet God does not heal everyone who trusts in Him by faith, as the other extreme suggests, then how is the believer to hold these two truths in tension, and what is the role of prayer in supernatural healing?

Point

The Bible is clear that God is the Creator of all things (Gen 1:1). Therefore, He can heal if He chooses to do so. In addition, Jesus and others in the Bible have divinely healed people in the past. The New Testament even spoke of people who had the gift of healing (1 Cor 12:9). Whether people with such gifts continue to exist today is a matter of dispute among many Bible interpreters, but the concern in this chapter is whether God supernaturally heals *at all* in today's world. In what follows, we will offer several Prayer

Principles to help the believer gain a balanced, biblical perspective on the role of prayer in supernatural healing.

Prayer Principle: God does not heal every person who prays; yet physical suffering can serve to accomplish God's will.

It is not God's will to heal everyone who is sick. When Timothy had stomach problems, Paul did not heal him or offer to heal him (1 Tim 5:23). Paul asked God to remove the thorn in his flesh, but God did not (2 Cor 12:7–10). Trophimus, another one of Paul's friends, was left sick in Miletus (2 Tim 4:20). Some people God chooses to use as a testimony of healing. God chooses to use other people as a testimony through their sufferings. Romans 8:23 teaches, "We ourselves who have the Spirit as the firstfruits—we also groan within ourselves, eagerly waiting for adoption, the redemption of our bodies."

The passages generally used by Prince and others who present the view that "God is not the God of disease" are ones that speak of God's redemptive work on the cross to forgive our sins. These verses are not speaking of physical well-being but rather the salvation of our souls. Jesus "was pierced because of our transgressions, crushed because of our iniquities" (Isa 53:5), but it was to provide ultimately for our salvation, not necessarily our physical healing. Jesus certainly cares about our physical health, but such verses do not prove He will never allow us to have sicknesses, disease, or disability as part of His divine plan. In misapplying Scripture related to Christ's sufferings on our behalf on the cross, Prince and others communicate not only an imbalanced view of divine healing but also an inaccurate understanding of Christ's work on the cross. On the contrary, as in the Bible, many godly people still suffer despite their great faith.

An excellent example of someone whose physical suffering has served to accomplish God's will is Joni Eareckson Tada. Limited to a wheelchair since high school, she has founded the ministry Joni and Friends, serving those affected by disability. She says:

> In a way I wish I could take to heaven my old, tattered Everest and Jennings wheelchair. I would point to the empty seat and say, "Lord, for decades I was paralyzed in this chair. But it showed me how paralyzed You must have felt to be nailed to Your Cross. My limitations taught me something about the limitations You endured when You laid aside your robes of state and put on the indignity of human flesh." At that point, with my strong and glorified body, I might sit in it, rub the armrests with my hands, look up at Jesus, and add, "The weaker I felt in this chair, the harder I leaned on You. And the harder I leaned, the more I discovered how strong You are. Thank you, Jesus, for learning obedience in your suffering. . . . You gave me grace to learn obedience in mine."[2]

God could have healed Joni from her disability, yet her disability has served as part of God's divine plan to change the lives of countless individuals who have been inspired by her story and outreach.

Another powerful example is the life of Randy Alcorn, a best-selling Christian author and speaker well known for his writings about heaven. As an adult he was diagnosed with diabetes. Reflecting on his initial diagnosis, he notes,

> When I became insulin-dependent, I wondered who wanted me ill, Satan or God. The obvious answer? Satan. But I'm also convinced, as was Paul, that the ultimate answer is God. Paul, under the inspiration of the Holy Spirit, saw God's sovereignty, grace, and humbling purpose of his disease (see 2 Cor 12:7–10). I have clearly and repeatedly seen the same in my own life.[3]

Rather than viewing his situation as one in which he lacked faith, Randy discovered that God was at work *through* his illness to transform his life and the lives of others. These few examples illustrate how some of the most virtuous Christians have faced extreme sickness or disease. While we do not fully understand why these things take place, we can take comfort in the fact that God can and does use such illnesses and diseases to glorify His name. Sometimes God chooses to rescue us from our sufferings; at other times He chooses to rescue us through our sufferings.

Prayer Principle: Satan's influence is under God's sovereignty, and no disease or sickness can attack our bodies without God's permission.

Can sickness be caused by a demon or Satan? On some occasions in the Bible, a demon was cast out and the person was restored to health as a result. For example, one young boy who could not speak or hear was healed when Jesus cast a spirit from him (Mark 9:24–27). However, there is no indication that all sickness is caused by the Devil or evil spirits. There may be some cases in which demons are to blame, but most sicknesses can be traced to germs, disease, or other explainable factors. God controls everything, and no disease or sickness can attack our bodies apart from God's permission.

Prayer Principle: God's Word reveals that healing is often part of His plan.

The same apostle Paul who wrote to Timothy regarding his stomach problems also wrote about another Christian man named Epaphroditus whom God healed:

> But I considered it necessary to send you Epaphroditus—
> my brother, coworker, and fellow soldier, as well as your
> messenger and minister to my need—since he has been
> longing for all of you and was distressed because you heard

that he was sick. Indeed, he was so sick that he nearly died. However, God had mercy on him, and not only on him but also on me, so that I would not have one grief on top of another. (Phil 2:25–27)

In this passage Paul specifically mentioned that Epaphroditus was healed due to "God's mercy." God intervened and provided healing; yet this healing was not something that would occur for every person in the Bible who developed an illness.

While I do not believe that anyone has the gift of healing, I do believe that God heals in answer to prayer, and I have seen great healings in answer to prayer. On April 25, 1985, more than 5,000 students at Liberty University fasted all day. All students committed themselves to pray for one hour for the healing of Vernon Brewer, the dean of students at the university, who had cancer. God healed Vernon. Each year on April 25, I call Vernon to praise God with him because God still heals. He needed both chemotherapy and radiation treatment for stomach cancer, plus an operation during which the doctors removed a five-pound cancerous tumor. But everyone knows what happened and agrees his recivert was not due to medical technology or anything the doctors did; it was a miracle of God![4]

Prayer Principle: Healing is God's plan for all believers even if it does not happen on this side of heaven.

Even when God does heal, that healing is only temporary. A person who is healed by God in this life does not receive a perfect, new body. We will not receive glorified bodies until sometime after this life when we are with the Lord. All physical healing in this life is therefore temporary. Those God heals will later become sick again or at the very least continue to age until death. The Bible does speak of the redemption of our bodies (Rom 8:23); yet only in the future with the Lord will we find ourselves in perfect health. Consider the following quote:

Sickness is certainly the result of the fall of man into sin, but God is very much in control, and He does indeed determine how far evil can go (just as He did with Satan and Job's trials—Satan was not allowed to exceed those boundaries). He tells us He is all-powerful over fifty times in the Bible, and it is amazing to see how His sovereignty unites with the choices we make (both bad and good) to work out His perfect plan (Rom 8:28).[5]

This eternal perspective helps the believer better understand those instances when God chooses not to heal. We can rest assured that there is a purpose. Romans 8:28 speaks of God's working "all things" for the good of those who love Him. Certainly, sickness and disease fall within this sweeping category of "all things." Mark Yarbrough notes,

> As with the Cross, our darkest hour may be God's finest moment. It may be there that he does his greatest work—albeit unseen to us. Thus instead of letting circumstances consume us, we are to be consumed with God. To that end, we pray without ceasing, trust in his sovereignty, and find comfort in his hope.[6]

Prayer Principle: Conditions for healing can bring about divine intervention.

James 5:13–16 is a key biblical text offering important parameters within which a believer can expect supernatural healing:

> Is anyone among you suffering? He should pray. . . . Is anyone among you sick? He should call for the elders of the church, and they should pray over him after anointing him with olive oil in the name of the Lord. The prayer of faith will save the sick person, and the Lord will restore

him to health; if he has committed sins, he will be forgiven. Therefore, confess your sins to one another and pray
for one another, so that you may be healed. (Jas 5:13–16)

There are eight key conditions in these verses which should inform
our biblical view of how to pray for healing. It is important, however, to keep a few qualifications in mind. First, this text more
narrowly addresses sickness and cannot necessarily be applied universally to all situations. Second, prayers for healing should not be
conducted apart from medical treatment. If you or the person you
are praying for has a serious illness, consult your doctor. *Prayer is
not to be used to replace medical treatment but to ask for God's healing in
addition to available medical treatment.* With this in mind, we turn
to our eight conditions according to James.

First, consider the role of God's judgment in the sickness.
This section on healing is introduced by the notion of judgment
in James 5:12: "So that you won't fall under judgment." In some
cases a sickness *could* be a judgment of God. When spiritual leaders
speak with a sick person, as difficult as it may be, it is important
to consider that God might be doing something through the infir-
mity as a means of bringing the individual to a place of repentance
and restoration.

Second, the sick person must initiate the process. Notice what
James said, "Is anyone among you suffering? He should pray"
(Jas 5:13). Then he says, "The prayer of faith will save the sick"
(Jas 5:15). Healing begins within the faith of the person who is
sick. When you pray for someone who is sick, I would encourage
you to use Scripture to build them up in their faith. The faith of
the sick person is an important part of the healing process.

Third, the elders (spiritual leaders) of the church must be
involved. Why does the Bible instruct us to call for the elders of
the church? These are the ones who have spiritual leadership over
the flock (Heb 13:7; 1 Tim 5:17). The text assumes a relationship

between the sick person and his or her spiritual leaders. It is important for church leaders to know the spiritual condition of the sick person, or any other condition that might prohibit their prayers from being answered. This allows church leaders to deal with the spiritual problem while medical professionals assist with the physical illness.

Fourth, the elders are called to use oil in praying for the sick. James explicitly refers to "anointing him with olive oil" (Jas 5:14). The translation "olive oil" is used in the HCSB version and a few other translations, while most other versions only use the word *oil*. Consequently, some have mistakenly translated the word *oil* as a metaphor, meaning the application of the work and person of the Holy Spirit to heal. In light of this spiritual interpretation, the actual use of oil becomes unnecessary. The Protestant Reformer John Calvin suggested that the *oil* was medicinal and that one of the church leaders was probably a medical doctor who used oil to cleanse the wound of impurities to facilitate healing. While the word *oil* could refer to any type of oil and God could heal without the use of oil, anointing the sick with oil serves as a symbolic act of faithful obedience to God.

Fifth, pray for the sick person audibly. While it is effective to pray silently, James seems to indicate that such prayers for the sick were spoken out loud. When the elders arrive and "pray over him" (Jas 5:14), they do so audibly. Something about an audible prayer captures the attention of God and draws in other petitioners. Jesus taught, "Again, I assure you: If two of you on earth agree about any matter that you pray for, it will be done for you by My Father in heaven" (Matt 18:19). Agreeing together usually includes audible communication. This suggests that the elders of the church agree together, as well as with the sick person, for healing.

Sixth, examine any possible connection between sickness and sin in the life of the individual and confess any known sin. Notice how James connects these two issues together: "The prayer of faith will save the sick person, and the Lord will restore him to health; if he has committed sins, he will be forgiven" (Jas 5:15). This passage seems to suggest that the sickness of the individual *could be* connected to sin in the person's life (though not always). In another place Paul suggests the same thing. In 1 Cor 11:29–30, for example, Paul teaches that those who had sinned in the process of taking Communion were sick, and some had even died.

The sick person must also confess his or her sins. James makes clear that a condition for healing includes confession of sins: "Confess your sins to one another and pray for one another, so that you may be healed" (Jas 5:16). This is another reason the person's local church leaders should be a part of the process. If sin is influencing the person's sickness, the spiritual leaders of the church can be involved when the sick person confesses sin and prays with them regarding spiritual needs.

Seventh, pray specifically for healing. Only one time in the Bible do we find the phrase, "the prayer of faith" (Jas 5:15). Many other times Christians are exhorted to have faith or exercise faith. But James specifically says, "The prayer of faith will save the sick person" (Jas 5:15). When we pray specifically, we stretch our faith to believe God for healing. However, when we pray vaguely such as, "Lord, bless the sick," or "Lord, do what they need," we fail to apply God's principles in this passage to pray specifically for healing. When we ask for specific healing, we can see God's answer when it takes place in response to our prayers.

Eighth, reestablish spiritual relationship with God. The Greek word for "prayer" in this passage is *proseuchomai*. It comes from the word *pros* that means "toward" and *euchomai* that implies "the face." Praying is a face-to-face relationship with God. In the same way, our goal is to help every person, especially those struggling with sickness, to draw close to the Lord and seek Him for strength.

Conclusion

The Bible encourages believers to pray for healing, and God's Word offers many examples of divine healing. Sometimes healing comes through medical means while at other times in ways that can only be described as miraculous. Yet God may also choose not to heal. Though many so-called "faith healers" have misrepresented the teachings of Scripture, God certainly has the power to heal in any way He chooses. Many cases of God's healing in miraculous ways are recorded throughout history and in the present.

Yet we must also realize that God's will may not include immediate, supernatural healing. In some cases He chooses to heal over time, while at other times sickness or disease even leads to death. Such circumstances still serve God's purposes in a manner we do not fully understand. Even Jesus did not heal every sick person during His earthly ministry. Examples of enduring sickness among faithful Christians can be found both in Scripture and in the present. As Joni Eareckson Tada writes:

> God can, and sometimes does, heal people in miraculous ways today, but the Bible does *not* teach that He will always heal those who come to Him in faith. His sovereignty reserves the right to heal or not to heal as He sees fit. For the person with the disability who does not experience healing, God will grant the strength to endure hardship. He will grant spiritual wisdom. Finally, He will reward those who are faithful, those who trust Him through affliction.[7]

A balanced biblical perspective is one that prays for God to heal, praises Him when He does, regardless of how the healing takes place, and acknowledges that God uses even suffering, disease, and disability for His glory.

Navigating this theological tension between God's ability to heal and His choice to withhold healing is difficult. The first step is to submit ourselves to God, asking for His will to be done as well as asking for wisdom regarding how to pray for the person in need. When we sense God is encouraging us to pray for healing in our own life or for someone else, we are to intercede in bold faith for His answer. Regardless of whether God ultimately heals as we expect, we can know that He hears our prayers and responds to our faith according to His perfect will.

Endnotes

1. Joseph Prince, "Health and Healing Confessions," JosephPrince. org, http://www.josephprince.org/Resources_Confess_The_Word_Health_And_Healing.html, accessed September 16, 2013. Emphasis added.

2. Joni Eareckson Tada, http://dailychristianquote.com/dcqtada.html, accessed October 10, 2008.

3. Randy Alcorn, "Is Healing Dependent upon Me Having Enough Faith?" EPM Ministries, http://www.epm.org/resources/2012/Aug/1/healing-dependent-upon-me-having-enough-faith, accessed August 1, 2012.

4. Elmer Towns, *Bible Answers for Almost All Your Questions* (Nashville, TN: Thomas Nelson, 2003), 221.

5. "Is It Sometimes God's Will for Believers to Be Sick?" Got Questions Ministries, http://www.gotquestions.org/sickness-will-God.html, accessed September 16, 2013.

6. Mark M. Yarbrough, "When God Doesn't Heal," *Christianity Today*, September 2004, vol. 48, no. 9, http://www.christianitytoday.com/ct/2004/september/30.80.html, accessed September 16, 2013.

7. Joni Eareckson Tada and Jack S. Oppenhuizen, "A Biblical Perspective on Healing," The Lausanne Movement, http://conversation.lausanne.org/en/resources/detail/12358#article_page_4, accessed July 7, 2012.

Chapter 5

Does God Answer Our Prayers Because We Are Persistent?

Elmer Towns

Anyone who has seen the classic movie *A Christmas Story* knows the plot of a small boy in a northern town continually begging for "an official Red Ryder Carbine-Action Two Hundred-Shot Range Model Air Rifle (BB gun) and this thing in the stock which tells time." Throughout the film, Ralphie begs for the Red Ryder BB gun. He writes letters, sneaks advertisements into his parents' magazines, and carefully crafts his petition to Santa Claus. In the end Ralphie does get his BB gun, feeling his efforts were worth the sacrifice.[1]

Similar to Ralphie's pursuit of his perfect Christmas gift, we should constantly bring our requests before our heavenly Father. Does it matter if we ask God one time for our request, or is it better to ask again and again, as Ralphie did, to help improve our odds for success? The Bible does reflect the value of persistent prayer. In 2 Cor 12:8, for example, Paul prayed three times for God to remove his "thorn in the flesh." He states, "I pleaded with the Lord three times to take it away from me." Yet Scripture also teaches that the heavenly Father knows what we need before we even ask. Matthew 6:8 reads: "Your Father knows the things you need before you ask Him."

There is an ongoing tension between those who think prayer is simply talking to God and those who treat prayer as intense negotiations with God to get what one asks. The tension often reflects a biblical and theological imbalance. In this chapter we will consider both perspectives, seeking the most accurate biblical understanding regarding this important aspect of prayer. First, we will address the view that God's answer to prayer is due, primarily, to our repetitive requests. Second, we will consider the pitfalls of overemphasizing this perspective and offer several Prayer Principles that reflect a more balanced biblical view of prayer and recognize the importance of a believer's praying before God in an ongoing manner that is part of an overall governing prayer relationship with Him.

Counterpoint

Does God answer our prayers simply due to our persistence? While on the surface few would deny that persistence in prayer is important, the problem with this view concerns the degree to which persistence becomes begging, inevitably taking on the character of negotiation with God. Yet the notion of begging carries with it several unfavorable connotations. For example, it suggests the use of emotions, manipulation, or insistence as means to receive something, or the idea of an inferior pleading to a superior for a benefit, as cancellation of punishment. Such a perspective seems to view the act of prayer from a purely human perspective. It is easy to allow personal experience to inform our view of God. In business, for example, negotiations are often made back and forth between two parties to obtain the best financial deal. In a legal settlement negotiations take place among lawyers to best provide for their clients.

Of course, in some circumstances begging is legitimate, such as when a person is in need of food or housing. In so far as believers understand their desperate need for God for even the most basic necessities, this legitimate sense is an appropriate analogy. Yet more often begging is illegitimate, such as the relentless child imploring his parents for candy at the checkout counter of a grocery store. This illegitimate sense is often applied to Christian prayer. If God says no the first time, keep trying. Additional attempts might include different tactics, increased emotion, or a variety of other options in the attempt to convince or persuade God that He should answer as the person has requested.

Yet those who view God in this manner neglect to realize that as a perfect Father, He answers perfectly *according to His will.* He might answer yes right away if the request is His will but would never answer yes if the request were not. However, often an answer from God comes at a time or in a way that is different than we originally anticipated. When this occurs, we need not conclude that God answered because we were persistent but rather that He answered our prayers according to His plan, in His way, and at His time.

Point

In contrast to the view of God that includes pleading with Him until He responds, a healthier biblical perspective views our persistent requests as part of an ongoing relationship, sustained by prayer, which submits our desires to the will of our heavenly Father. Below are several Prayer Principles that reflect a more balanced biblical view of prayer.

Prayer Principle: Persistence in prayer is based on our relationship with God.

Jesus taught that persistence was one of the key characteristics of prayer. The Bible suggests that Jesus prayed for long periods of time. The reference in Luke 11:1, for example, suggests continuous action ("He was praying . . ."). His disciples believed His spiritual power came from Jesus' time with the Father, so they asked, "Lord, teach us to pray" (Luke 11:1). Jesus offered a two-part answer. First, He reminded them to pray what is referred to as the Lord's Prayer.

Second, Jesus told them a story of a man who had unexpected guests arrive late at night. The man did not have any food to feed his visitors. Americans rarely understand the Middle Eastern cultural passion for hospitality, so it is easy to miss the extreme embarrassment of the situation. In desperation the man ran to a neighbor's home, knocked on the door, and asked him to wake up. "Hey, I need three loaves of bread to feed my special guests." "Go away," the voice behind the locked door replied. "I'm in bed and my family is asleep." Yet the neighbor persisted, "I really need to borrow some food!" "Go away," the irritated voice from inside continued. Jesus' application of the story is significant. He states, "Even though he won't get up and give him anything because he is his friend, yet because of his friend's persistence, he will get up and give him as much as he needs" (Luke 11:8).

Did this needy man keep knocking because this was the only house in the village? Probably not. There were likely many other houses in the town, and some of his neighbors might have still been awake. This man was persistent at the home of his friend because *he knew the heart of his friend*. A relationship characterized by mutual trust allowed him to knock persistently expecting a response. Jesus used this story as an example of how we can come to God with the expectation that He desires to help those who persistently ask Him for their needs. E. M. Bounds states,

> Persistence . . . is a condition of prayer. We are to press the matter, not with vain repetitions, but with urgent repetitions. We repeat, not to count the times, but to gain the prayer. We cannot quit praying because heart and soul are in it. We pray "with all perseverance." We hang to our

prayer because by them we live. We press our pleas because we must have them or die.[2]

Expect God to respond in a way that is consistent with your relationship to Him.

Prayer is based on our relationship to the Father. We are His children because we are born again into His family (John 1:12–13; 3:1–8). Therefore, we begin our prayers as Jesus instructs us, "Our Father in heaven" (Matt 6:9). Just as an earthly father has an obligation to provide for the needs of the child he brings into the world, so we can trust our heavenly Father to hear when we bring our needs to Him. We can trust our Father to take care of us. Matthew 6:31–32 states, "So don't worry, saying, 'What will we eat?' or 'What will we drink?' or 'What will we wear?' For the idolaters eagerly seek all these things, and your heavenly Father knows that you need them." If we fail to bring our needs to our heavenly Father, we doubt His care for us, and doubt weakens our relationship with God.

Several other biblical passages reflect an important link between persistent prayer and a relationship with God. In John 15:3, 5, for example, Jesus told His disciples that fruitfulness depends on the Christian who will "abide in Me." The relationship between the vine and branches, sustained through prayer, is necessary to produce fruit. When we remain attached to the Lord, God will truly care for and protect us. Given this important link between prayer and relationship, we must sustain our connection to God through persistent prayer.

In yet another passage, a woman from Canaan came to Christ and said, "Have mercy on me. . . . My daughter is cruelly tormented by a demon" (Matt 15:22). Jesus did not respond immediately, but after her persistence He granted her request. Our Lord's attitude was intended to test her faith. Jesus rewarded her with the miraculous healing of her daughter. We can observe that our prayers may often not be answered immediately simply because God is testing our faith. God may desire that we persist in our requests for some needs before He responds.[3]

Prayer Principle: Persistence leads to dependence.

Trust is one of the most basic elements characterizing the relationship between Christians and God. We must put all our trust—our dependence—on our heavenly Father. Proverbs 3:5–6 states, "Trust in the LORD with all your heart, and do not rely on your own understanding; think about Him in all your ways, and He will guide you on the right paths." When Jesus told His followers, "Whatever you ask in My name, I will do it so that the Father may be glorified in the Son" (John 14:13), He was modeling for us an elementary form of dependence on Him. As the believer continues to ask, our dependence is deepened and enriched.

Most of us desire independence. The unsaved heart is especially rebellious against the moral rules of God. We want to "live and let live" without intervention from others. But God has a different requirement. Jesus said, "If anyone wants to come with Me, he must deny himself, take up his cross daily, and follow Me" (Luke 9:23). Therefore, continually following Christ in humble dependency is the essence of Christianity. Continued prayer is one exercise where we show our trust in Him. When we keep on asking for the things that we need, we are deepening that dependence on God.

What is dependence on God, and why is it important? In Matt 6:25–34, Jesus taught a parable which provides six principles about dependence.[4] First, God teaches us to depend on Him by revealing His power to supply our food and clothing. Verse 26 shares, "Look at the birds of the sky: They don't sow or reap or gather into barns, yet your heavenly Father feeds them." Second, the God who cares for birds cares even more for us. The phrase, "Aren't you worth more than they?" clearly explains God's feelings for us. He loves us and considers us of great value in His sight. As a result, we are to trust in Him. Third, worry needlessly wastes energy. Verse 27 reads, "Can any of you add a single cubit to his height by worrying?" Worry does not add value to our relationship with God; it takes away from it. Fourth, worry ignores the reality of God's faithfulness in our lives. Verse 30 instructs, "If that's how God clothes the grass of the field, which is here today and thrown into the furnace tomorrow, won't He do much more for you—you of little faith?" Here Jesus presents worry in contrast with faith. Increased dependence on God leads to less worry.

Fifth, Jesus clearly teaches that we are God's children and part of His family. As Jesus does throughout the Sermon on the Mount, He refers to God as our heavenly Father: "Your heavenly Father knows that you need them" (v. 32). God's care for us is exhibited through a father-child relationship that stands as a strong relational bond and urges us to trust in Him. Finally, worry about tomorrow causes us to miss out on God's purposes for us today. Verses 33–34 share, "But seek first the kingdom of God and His righteousness, and all these things will be provided for you. Therefore don't worry about tomorrow, because tomorrow will worry about itself. Each day has enough trouble of its own." Jesus did not belittle the problems we face but placed them in perspective. When God is our Father, we need not worry about tomorrow because He is in full control. We can confidently depend on Him. All six of these principles help us better understand God's desire for our dependence on Him.

Prayer Principle: Persistence in prayer grows our love for God and draws us into His plan.

The first two Prayer Principles are incomplete without this one. The Father enjoys it when His children ask things from Him as a reflection of their love. Even in the movie *A Christmas Story*, Ralphie's father enjoyed his son's pursuit for the Red Ryder BB gun. Most of all Ralphie's dad enjoyed the excitement on Ralphie's face when he opened his present and found his much-anticipated gift. In the same way God takes great pleasure in answering our prayers. He is not a begrudging god who reluctantly gives in to the requests of his children only after they have groveled and begged. God wants us to ask Him for our needs because He likes to be asked. If you are a father or mother, you probably enjoy it when your child asks for something rather than demanding it. Parents who love their children desire to provide for their needs. Likewise, our Lord appreciates when we ask Him to meet our needs as much as He appreciates providing for those needs through His strength.

Our love for God and His pleasure to respond grow in an atmosphere of asking and receiving. We do not continually pray for something because we want to wear down God's resistance. Instead, we remain in His presence because we love Him. When God gives us the privilege of asking Him for our needs, He invites us into partnership with Him as He fulfills His plan. God has a plan for each of us, and He wants us to fulfill that plan. That plan involves our dependence on Him, but it also involves serving Him in loving obedience. When we study God's Word, help the poor, or serve in our local church, we enter into partnership with God. To be successful in anything we do, we must persistently pray for God's blessing on our endeavor. We must pray for God's work in the hearts of those we are serving. We must pray for God's anointing on the things we do for Him. Continual prayer enriches our service for Him.

Prayer Principle: We are called to persist in prayer even when God is silent because that allows God to work in the life of the one who prays.

Those who view prayer simply as begging miss out on the bigger picture of the role of persistent prayer in the life of the one who prays. God wants His children to keep on asking even though He does not answer immediately because He wants to change the one who prays. God calls us to, "Keep asking, and it will be given to you. Keep searching, and you will find. Keep knocking, and the door will be opened to you" (Luke 11:9). In such cases where God prolongs His answer, our persistence in prayer is not about getting God to do something He does not want to do but about working in the life of the one who prays. Scripture offers several ways we are changed through persistent prayer.

First, we grow closer to God by spending time in His presence. You have probably heard the saying, "Prayer changes things." This is true, but prayer also changes us. God often doesn't immediately answer because we need to grow closer to Him. The Father wants us to spend time with Him. He says, "Seek My face" (Ps 27:8). When we see a command to seek God, He's not suggesting we beg for answers. Instead, it's for our benefit—to grow deeper in our walk with Him (Pss 9:10; 14:2; 63:1). The Father in heaven desires our worship (see John 4:23). If He does not answer our prayers as quickly as we would like, we stay in His presence until we find His response.

Second, when we do not receive an instant answer to prayer, we are forced to deal with potential sin in our lives. David prayed, "Search me, God" (Ps 139:23). In God's presence we face God's searchlight, and He reveals our sin. God often shows us our hidden sins during these times, and we pray, "Cleanse me from any hidden faults" (Ps 19:12).

Third, during times of waiting for the Lord's response to our prayer, we learn what we have not been doing as a Christian. Sometimes God lets us continue to ask Him for our requests because He wants us to learn certain lessons before He answers. In my own personal life I have prayed for things I was too immature to have. God has us wait in His presence so we can learn that which we do not know. He may wait for us to study His Word (2 Tim 2:15), meditate on His Word (Josh 1:8), fast (Matt 6:16), give financially (1 Cor 16:1–2), share our faith with an unbeliever (2 Cor 5:11), serve someone in need (Luke 9:23), or walk through an open door (1 Cor 16:9).

Fourth, persistent prayer in the face of God's silence helps shape our prayers around the will of God. God will not answer a prayer that is against His will or His ways. Even the apostle Paul did not get every prayer request answered the way he desired. He prayed, "Brothers, my heart's desire and prayer to God concerning them is for their salvation!" (Rom 10:1). Despite his prayers many Jewish people rejected Jesus as the Messiah. Paul also prayed three times for God to remove an unknown thorn from his flesh (2 Cor 12:7–9), but God did not do it.

Fifth, when God prolongs His answer to our prayers, we cultivate patience to trust God's timing. We are impatient people. Our favorite word is *now*, and we want God to answer our prayers immediately. Yet God might have us wait because He knows the thing we want will take time to deliver. God wants us to trust Him from the first time we pray for something until we get an answer, which sometimes means a long wait. During the wait we must continue praying.

The Scriptures clearly illustrate this principle of patiently waiting on God's timing. In Daniel 10, for example, we are told that the prophet prayed for twenty-one days, but the answer was blocked by an evil spirit during this time: "From the first day that you . . . humble yourself before your God, your prayers were heard. . . . But the prince of the kingdom of Persia opposed me for 21 days" (Dan 10:12–13). Sometimes our spiritual enemies work to block our prayers from being answered. When this happens, we do not stop praying but continue until God's answer is provided.

Another example is Elijah's persistent prayers for rain. James 5:17–18 states, "Elijah was a man with a nature like ours; yet he prayed earnestly that it would not rain. . . . Then he prayed again, and the sky gave rain." But look carefully how God answered. Elijah "bowed down on the ground and put his face between his knees" (1 Kgs 18:42). He sent his servant to see if rain was coming and "there's nothing" (1 Kgs 18:42). Elijah kept praying until the answer came: "On the seventh time, he [the servant] reported, 'There's a cloud as small as a man's hand coming from the sea'" (1 Kgs 18:44). God answered Elijah's prayer through the development of a natural weather pattern: "The sky grew dark with clouds and wind, and there was a downpour" (1 Kgs 18:45).

God may not immediately save a loved one for whom you are praying. It may take time for someone to witness to them, or it may take time for them to lose those things keeping them from God. God is often at work in our lives even when we do not see results or understand what He is doing. This does not mean we should stop! It should encourage us to continue praying.

Conclusion

To some people prayer is simply pleading or begging for answers from God. When God does not answer, the response is to continue pleading until God gives in. As we have seen, the problem with this perspective is that it views God from a human perspective rather than as our perfect heavenly Father. God is not too busy for us, nor does He wait until we cry louder or more frequently. In fact, everything God does for us is for our good. As best-selling author Philip Yancey illustrates:

> I remember my first visit to Old Faithful in Yellowstone National park. Rings of Japanese and German tourists surrounded the geyser, their video cameras trained like weapons on the famous hole in the ground. A large digital clock stood beside the spot, predicting twenty-four minutes before the eruption.
>
> My wife and I passed the countdown in the dining room of Old Faithful Inn overlooking the geyser. When the digital clock reached one minute, we, along with every other diner, left our seats and rushed to the windows to see the big, wet event.
>
> I noticed immediately, as if on signal, a crew of busboys and waiters descended on the tables to refill water glasses and clear away dirty dishes. When the geyser went off, we tourists oohed and aahed and clicked our cameras;

a few spontaneously applauded. But, glancing back over my shoulder, I saw that not a single waiter or busboy—not even those who had finished their chores—looked out the huge windows. Old Faithful, grown entirely too familiar, had lost its power to impress them.[5]

We often miss this aspect of God's faithfulness when we pray. We focus on the how-to rather than on our heavenly Father. However, prayer is a relationship between God and His children. Through prayer we worship God and enjoy fellowship with Him. We bring our needs to the Lord and ask Him to meet them according to His will. Investing time in God's presence is not work to help prove God should answer us; time in God's presence is something we enjoy and anticipate, looking forward to the day when we enjoy perfect eternity with Him in heaven.

If God says no or does not answer when we wish, it does not mean He loves us less or has not heard our prayer. Instead, we discover that God's plans are often different from ours yet are perfect and infinitely better than our desires. George Müller, a nineteenth-century Christian leader, is known by Christian historians as a man of great faith and prayer. Part of his success in prayer was his intense and repetitive intercession to God based on his faith that God would eventually answer if he continued in prayer. Müller began early in his ministry praying for five friends to come to faith in Christ. One man became a Christian after several months of prayer. Two of the other men trusted Christ following ten years of intercession. A fourth man came to know the Lord after twenty-five years of intercession. Right up until his death, Müller did not give up praying for the fifth man. At Müller's funeral, fifty-two years after he began praying for his five unsaved friends, the last of the five men was saved. While we seek to bring every need before our God, we trust Him to respond as He knows best, trusting in Him as our Father who expresses His responses to us out of His perfect nature and love.

Endnotes

1. *A Christmas Story*, directed by Bob Clark (Metro Golden Mayer, 1983), DVD (MGM Home Entertainment, 1997).

2. E. M. Bounds, *Purpose in Prayer*, Christian Classics Ethereal Library, http://www.ccel.org/ccel/bounds/purpose.VI.html, accessed September 16, 2013.

3. Elmer Towns, *Bible Answers for Almost All Your Questions* (Nashville, TN: Thomas Nelson, 2003), 219.

4. Kenneth Boa, "Dependence on God," Bible.org, http://bible.org /seriespage/dependence-god, accessed September 16, 2013.

5. Philip Yancey, "What Surprised Jesus," *Christianity Today*, September 12, 1994, 88.

Chapter 6

Can You Pray to a God You Think May Not Be There?

Alex McFarland

H ave you ever dropped your quarters into a vending machine slot and had the unfortunate experience of watching your potato chips bag tumble from the little spiral rack only to become wedged between the glass and the shelf? Your first response was probably frustration, followed by a few choice words and some light tapping on the glass. If that did not resolve the situation, you might have rocked the machine back and forth a time or two, hoping to dislodge that bag of salty goodness from its lofty perch. You may have even attempted to buy another bag of chips, hoping that the weight of the second might fall on the first and dislodge the offending snack. If all exertion yielded nothing, you probably walked away grumbling under your breath about being cheated by the stupid vending machine.

Many people view God and prayer like their interaction with the errant vending machine. They insert their quarter (prayer) into the slot on the vending machine and push the button, expecting their product. When they do not get their selection (their desired answer to the prayer), frustration ensues. Anger follows before they begin beating and banging on the ceiling of heaven. Eventually, disappointment sets in, and they walk away complaining that somehow God is unfair for not giving them what they want and feel they deserve. Some might conclude from this experience that since their prayers went unanswered, God does not exist—which is about as illogical as saying that the vending machine does not exist because it did not deliver the potato chips. In this chapter we will assess the argument of those who question the existence of God based on unanswered prayer. Next we will counter their argument with several Prayer Principles regarding God's purposes in prayer and the staggering evidence for the efficacy of prayer. We will conclude with several observations regarding God's nature as it relates to prayer.

Counterpoint

Skeptics of Christianity often make the claim that if God does not answer every prayer then He must not exist. When a believer points out that God does answer every prayer, just not necessarily with the desired answer, the skeptic will mockingly retort with a few Scripture verses taken out of context to try to disprove God's existence.

As proof of their position, skeptics point to various clinical studies conducted in medical facilities on the effects of intercessory prayer. Their purpose in quoting these studies is to provide empirical, measurable evidence that prayer does not work and therefore God does not exist. Indeed some studies conducted in years past have shown that intercessory prayer had little or no effect on the patients that were prayed for. (We'll discuss the validity of these studies later in the chapter.) But does that necessarily mean we can conclude that God is nonexistent?

If you dig deep enough into the life of a skeptic, you will probably find a wound of some kind that they have blamed on

God. They may have earnestly prayed about a particular situation—perhaps for the healing of a loved one—but did not receive the desired answer to their prayer. Instead of becoming better, their relative became worse or even died. Their hurt and anger over God's failure to answer their prayer led them to abandon their faith in God or conclude that God is merely a distant observer who either doesn't care about their personal life or is powerless to intervene.

Point

God's existence does not depend on the actions He does or does not take. He is not the cosmic vending machine that skeptics, and even some Christians, have made Him out to be. A skeptic often approaches the subject of prayer with the presupposition that God does not exist, which leads them to conclude that prayer is little more than pointless superstition. If you were to produce a verifiable instance of answered prayer, they would most certainly dismiss it, attributing the result to coincidence or wishful thinking rather than supernatural intervention.

Prayer is not magic either. No secret combination of words will ensure an affirmative response from God. No mystical number of repetitions of a prayer will bring about a change in God's answer when He chooses to say no or "not yet." Those who view prayer as nothing more than a tool to obtain instant gratification understand neither prayer nor the God from whom they expect an answer.

Many sincere seekers at some point become disheartened when God doesn't answer yes to their prayers. A child may not understand why a parent says no or "not yet" and may respond with a petulant, "You don't love me!" Only maturity, experience, and a good deal of hindsight can reveal the wisdom in the answer from the parent. But some have a much more difficult time accepting that God does say no or "not yet" to our prayers for reasons that are not immediately clear to us. There is a profound lack of patience to see what else He might have in mind through His answer. Below are several Prayer Principles describing how the purpose and efficacy of prayer continues to manifest the existence of God.

Prayer Principle: Prayer is primarily about maturing our faith.

If unbelievers and Christians see prayer exclusively as a means by which they obtain stuff, then they have clearly missed the whole point of the practice. Prayer is first and foremost a relational practice in which God's children communicate with their heavenly Father in a personal way. Christians understand prayer to be two-way communication; we speak to our Father and listen for His still small voice. The primary focus of Christian prayer is to mature in our relationship with God.

It is clear from Scripture that prayer was intended to be an intimate practice. Jesus said in Matt 6:6, "But when you pray, go into your private room, shut your door, and pray to your Father who is in secret. And your Father who sees in secret will reward you." Some have wrongly interpreted this verse as a prohibition against public prayer, but that is not the meaning of the verse. Jesus is teaching us that the practice of prayer is not to gain favor with men—as the hypocrites of His day assumed—but to commune with God. When we meet with God in secret, we are able to shut out the distractions of the world and focus our attention completely on Him. When we make prayer more about getting to know God rather than getting answers to prayer, God has promised that He will reward us openly (Matt 6:4).

The relational nature of prayer is difficult for the skeptic to understand. As a husband, I am under no obligation to buy another woman a diamond necklace simply because she asks me. If I did, I am sure my wife would have something to say about it! A father is under no obligation to buy a toy for any child other than his own. The skeptic is asking, even demanding, a complete stranger to dole out goodies to the kiddies by saying that God has to answer every prayer just because He exists and is a benevolent God.

Prayer Principle: God is not obligated to answer the prayers of unbelievers.

God is under no obligation to answer the prayers of those who do not have a personal relationship with Him through Jesus Christ. Scripture says that "anyone who turns his ear away from hearing the law—even his prayer is detestable" (Prov 28:9). The apostle Peter wrote, "For the eyes of the Lord are on the righteous, and his ears are open to their prayer. But the face of the Lord is against those who do evil" (1 Pet 3:12 ESV).

This does not mean God never answers their prayers. Indeed, there are biblical instances where God answered the prayers of unbelievers—especially those connected with repentance. The Ninevites (unbelievers) repented at the preaching of Jonah, and God spared their city (Jonah 3:5–10). In Acts 10, a Roman Centurion named Cornelius, who was noted as a devout man who feared God, gave to charity and prayed daily. God sent him a vision to call for Simon Peter, who came to the house of the soldier, shared the gospel with Cornelius, and baptized him. As a general rule, however, He does not answer the prayers of those who have not placed their faith in Him through His Son Jesus Christ.

In Acts 19, we read about an incident where some itinerant Jewish exorcists were going around attempting to cast out demons by invoking the name of Jesus Christ over demon-possessed people. They had undoubtedly seen how God used Paul to heal the sick and cast out evil spirits (see Acts 19:11–12). The Bible says:

> Then some of the itinerant Jewish exorcists attempted to pronounce the name of the Lord Jesus over those who had evil spirits, saying, "I command you by the Jesus that Paul preaches!" Seven sons of Sceva, a Jewish chief priest, were doing this. The evil spirit answered them, "I know Jesus, and I recognize Paul—but who are you?" Then the man who had the evil spirit leaped on them, overpowered them

all, and prevailed against them, so that they ran out of that house naked and wounded. (Acts 19:13–16)

These men suffered the consequences of their presumptuous prayer. The demon essentially told these men, "I don't have to take any orders from you because you are not one of God's children." Unlike Paul, the seven sons of Sceva were absolutely no threat to the kingdom of darkness. Since they lacked a personal relationship with God, these men did not even appear on hell's radar screen.

Prayer Principle: God answers prayer according to His will and not ours.

Yet what do we say in the case of a godly saint who does have an intimate relationship with God and prays to be healed from cancer but does not receive healing? Did God fail because He did not heal? What if God's purposes are better served by not healing that saint? What if the suffering of this child of God works to draw her and her family closer to their heavenly Father? What if the grace and patience displayed by this sickly saint leads to a family member's embracing the gospel? The Bible says:

> We have also received an inheritance in Him, predestined according to the purpose of the One *who works out every-thing in agreement with the decision of His will*, so that we who had already put our hope in the Messiah might bring praise to His glory. (Eph 1:11–12, emphasis added)

God answers every Christian's prayer according to His will and not our own. Ultimately, God is glorified in the life of a believer even if He says no or wait.

The believer, who has intimate knowledge of God's heart, understands that God sees the beginning and the end of all situations and always acts in a way that accomplishes His purpose.

Regardless of the answer received, the believer learns to trust God through the experience of prayer even if the answer to that prayer is different than what was expected or hoped for.

This means God may answer our prayers according to our desires, or He may change our desires to be in line with His will. We may pray repeatedly for a certain outcome but through our openness and desire to know Him through Scripture, we may discover that our desires are simply ours, not His. His will then becomes clear, and our desires change to match His will, thereby changing our prayer.

The apostle Paul is the perfect example of this. In 2 Corinthians 12, Paul speaks of a heavenly vision that was given to him from God wherein he was caught up into the third heaven and saw and heard many things that were inexpressible and difficult for him to speak about. After the experience Paul says he was given a "thorn in the flesh" in order to keep him from becoming conceited as a result of having received such a glorious vision from God. Scripture does not explicitly identify the nature of this "thorn," but most assume it was a painful medical problem. Whatever the condition, it drove Paul to intense prayer:

> Concerning this, I pleaded with the Lord three times to take it away from me. But He said to me, "My grace is sufficient for you, for power is perfected in weakness." Therefore, I will most gladly boast all the more about my weaknesses, so that Christ's power may reside in me. (2 Cor 12:8–9)

We know from Scripture that Paul repeatedly received answers to his prayers. Yet in this instance Paul did not receive healing. Instead, he received deeper insight from God in the matter as the Lord assured him that "His grace was sufficient" for the situation.

Paul did not abandon his faith when the answer was no; instead, he grew spiritually closer to God because of the no.

Indeed, a believer can learn much about God when his request is denied if he is willing to ask God and listen. James reminds us that whenever we go through various trials, "the testing of your faith produces endurance," and if we lack wisdom about our trials, we should "ask God, who gives to all generously and without criticizing, and it will be given to him" (Jas 1:3, 5).

The skeptic might see this answer as a Christian cop-out, an excuse for God's not acting. They will point an accusing finger and say, "See, Jesus said, 'Whatever you ask the Father in My name, He will give you' [John 15:16] but Jesus did not do it!" (I will address this issue more in chapter 7.) They are unable to understand fully because they do not know God intimately. In addition, they overlook what the entirety of Scripture teaches regarding prayer as opposed to isolated texts taken out of context.

In considering the skeptic who appeals to "statistical proof" from research studies on prayer, one might question, since prayer is primarily tied to intimacy with God and maturing our faith, can the efficacy of Christian prayer be completely and accurately measured in a research study? What results are we looking for to prove the effectiveness of prayer through these prayer studies? Is complete healing the only criteria acceptable to skeptics? Is it even possible to design a study that takes into account all of the variables involved? Below are just a few of these variables.

First, how do we know people in a control group are not receiving prayer from other relatives and friends? What if one of the preconditions of the study is that the intercessor must have a close relationship with the Lord since Jesus said, "If you remain in Me and My words remain in you, ask whatever you want and it will be done for you" (John 15:7)? How can one verify the vitality of the intercessor's relationship with God? Is some quantitative score placed on a person's prayer life?

Second, what kind of time frame is sufficient to put on such a study? Is praying for fourteen days enough to produce quantifiable results? How about twenty-eight? How about six months? Will follow-up be conducted after the patient's discharge to determine if healing occurred later? God does not necessarily operate on our time frame; neither can our sovereign God be manipulated into bending His will to ours.

Third, consider the fact that sometimes people who seek healing have to confess and repent of their sins prior to receiving their healing. Can a research study account for this variable? One example found in the Bible is the story of the four men who brought their paralytic friend to Jesus to be healed. After they failed because of the crowds to enter the house where Jesus was teaching, they improvised and took him up on the roof, peeled back the layers of thatch, and lowered him down into the presence of Jesus. What happened next came as a big shock to the crowd. Mark wrote: "Seeing their faith, Jesus told the paralytic, 'Son, your sins are forgiven'" (Mark 2:5).

Jesus went beyond the man's obvious symptoms to the root cause of his ailment—which in this case appears to be his sin. When the people in the crowd began to question whether Jesus had the authority to forgive sins, Jesus said, "But so you may know that the Son of Man has authority on earth to forgive sins, I tell you: get up, pick up your mat, and go home" (Mark 2:10–11). Scripture says that he immediately arose, took his bed, and walked out in plain sight of everyone. Forgiveness of his sin was one of the limiting factors that prevented his healing prior to this encounter with Jesus.

Prayer Principle: Millions of answered prayers can't be a fluke.

Of course, God's answers to prayer are not limited to the realm of physical healing. Those who are skeptical of prayer have to contend with the eyewitness testimony of the millions of saints throughout the church age who have prayed to God for guidance, provision, the salvation of loved ones, and deliverance from sin among other things, and have received answers to their prayers.

George Müller was known as a man of great faith who received numerous answers to prayer throughout his many years of ministry. Müller was led by God to start several orphanages in Bristol completely by faith without going into debt or appealing to donors for funding. He simply prayed for God's provision and expected God to answer. His diaries document around 50,000 answers to prayer, 30,000 of which were received within twenty-four hours of the request being made.[1]

On one occasion Müller had the orphans sit down at the table for breakfast in front of empty plates and bowls in spite of the fact that there was nothing to eat. Müller prayed and thanked God for the food they were about to receive. When he finished praying, the baker knocked on the door. He had spent most of the night in sleeplessness, burdened that the orphans might not have enough to eat, so he had come to give the orphans enough fresh bread to meet their need. Immediately afterwards, the milkman knocked on the door and gave the children a supply of fresh milk. It seems that his cart had broken down in front of the orphanage, and he did not want the milk to go to waste.

Later in Müller's ministry, God opened the door for him to travel extensively and preach on prayer. He traveled around 200,000 miles completely on faith as he had done for many years running the orphanages of Bristol. On one voyage Müller was on board the ship *Sardinian* bound for North America. Müller needed to be in Quebec for a preaching engagement the following Saturday afternoon. The ship ran into a dense fogbank just off the coast of Newfoundland that slowed their progress dramatically. Müller went to the captain to inform him of his need to be in Quebec on time. The captain responded that it would be impossible given the foggy conditions. Müller suggested that they go to the chart room to pray, but the captain, an unbeliever, thought Müller was out of his mind. When the captain tried to point out the density of the fog to Müller, he responded by saying, "My eye is not on the density of the fog, but on the living God, who controls every circumstance of my life." Müller proceeded to take the matter to God in prayer. When he finished praying, Müller invited the captain to open the door where he found that the fog had indeed lifted.[2]

I have personally witnessed God answer prayer. Recently I was invited to preach a series of revival meetings at a church. The pastor was deeply concerned for his unbelieving sister who had lived a sinful lifestyle for most of her life. The pastor got word that she was on her deathbed, so he left for Texas to be with her on the day I arrived to lead the services. Meanwhile, the church began praying for her salvation during the five days of revival. I even encouraged people to fast as they prayed. We received word that in a moment of consciousness, she called for her brother and said, "I need to talk to Don. He can help me get right with God." She prayed to receive Christ and within a few days lapsed back into a coma and passed away. Needless to say there was major rejoicing for the answer to prayer in that church. I truly believe our intense intercession for this woman played a role in her conversion.

A friend who is an evangelist and pastor often shares the story of an answered prayer from his first international mission trip in 1999. He and a team from his church were staying in a hotel in Brasov, Romania, while leading a vacation Bible school outreach with one of the local Baptist churches. One of the youth had met a young lady in the hotel lobby and struck up a conversation with her. She was interested in him as more than a friend, but he was concerned for her salvation and wanted to share the gospel with her. After their conversation ended, she went up to her room for the evening, and he walked outside in search of my evangelist friend. This youth told my friend of his desire to witness to this young lady again. He requested prayer that God would give him another opportunity to talk with this girl, so they immediately prayed. After the prayer the youth walked back into the hotel lobby where he found the girl standing alone. When he saw her, he asked, "I thought you were going to go upstairs to your room for the night?" She replied, "I was, but something told me that I needed to go back downstairs, so I did." He got his opportunity to share the gospel with her again.

Conclusion

In this chapter we have argued that God's purposes in prayer as well as the staggering evidence for the efficacy of prayer point to the existence of a benevolent God. The answers to the prayers of millions of saints both past and present are too numerous and wonderful to dismiss as coincidence or wishful thinking. Christians know that God answers prayer, and even if the answer to their prayer is "no," "wait," or "I have something better in mind," that answer will always work to serve His purposes of strengthening a believer's relationship with God. Prayer is a vital part of maturing a believer's faith. It is a family privilege, an intimate dialogue between a loving Father and His adopted children, which leads them to grow deeper in their love for the One who rescued them from the consequences of their sin and made them to be joint heirs with His Son Jesus Christ. Without that vital connection to God, prayer will seem to be a pointless act. When one lacks biblical understanding of the purpose of prayer, it will seem like nothing more to a person than pushing a button on a vending machine in search of instant gratification.

Endnotes

1. "The Work of Müller's," http://www.mullers.org/heritage/the workofmullers.htm, accessed September 16, 2013.

2. "The Bristol Miracle," http://www.mullers.org/component /docman/doc_download/2-the-bristol-miracle.

Chapter 7

Can Prayer Do Anything Because God Can Do Anything?

Alex McFarland

I f God can do anything, then can we as believers do anything God can do through prayer? The Bible seems to indicate that the prayers of believers who ask in faith will not go unanswered. On the one hand are those who doubt such a claim, noting that there has never been a healing of an amputee or an actual mountain moved. Are there limits to what we can pray for and still be biblical? On the other hand are those who believe that the efficacy of prayer extends to health, wealth, and prosperity but is subject to the faith of the believer. Can a believer, for example, pray for a better parking spot when shopping at the local mall or for apple pie at their favorite restaurant instead of coconut cream? In addition, does the answer to prayer depend on the amount of faith you have? In this chapter we will critique this latter view, commonly referred to as the "prosperity" gospel, offering several Prayer Principles that reflect a more balanced, biblical view of the nature and purpose of prayer.

Counterpoint

Every Sunday morning in America, millions of Christians tune their television sets to watch their favorite television preacher while they prepare to attend their local church. Many find comfort in the teachings of well-known and respected Bible teachers such as Charles Stanley or David Jeremiah. Others tune in to watch local church services led by lesser known but still faithful men of God. Some tune in to watch a different kind of preacher—one who teaches his followers that God does not want them to be poor but to prosper, not to be sick but to be healthy. They teach and preach that if a believer has enough faith, God will bless them with more than enough money to pay their bills, buy nice things, and drive the best cars. Through faith any believer can live the American Dream and prosper.

These TV preachers certainly stand as a shining example of the theology they expound. They wear the finest clothing, drive luxury cars, and fly off in their personal jets whenever they have a speaking engagement. When they are not traveling or preaching, they retire to a multimillion-dollar gated estate where they enjoy the "blessings" of God. All of these blessings are attributed to their positive confession of faith and to the goodness of God who is just waiting on the threshold of heaven for believers to ask so they might receive.

The "prosperity gospel," as some have called it, has found a willing audience of viewers and listeners. In 2006, *Time* magazine ran an article titled, "Does God Want You to Be Rich?" For the article *Time* surveyed 770 professing Christians and discovered that 61 percent of those being polled agreed with the statement, "God wants people to be financially prosperous," while only 26 percent disagreed.[1] Sales for books written by these ministers have been phenomenal. One of the leading proponents of prosperity theology is Pastor Joel Osteen. Two of his most successful books, *Your Best Life Now: 7 Steps to Living at Your Full Potential* and *Become a Better*

You: 7 Keys to Improving Your Life Every Day, topped out *The New York Times* Best Seller list, selling millions of copies.

Point

If the teachings of the prosperity gospel are valid, are believers missing out on God's blessing simply because they do not have enough faith to ask for bigger and better stuff? Can we "name and claim" our way to getting out of debt and enjoying a life free from sickness and suffering? Or do we have reason to be skeptical? We believe such a view misunderstands prayer on the most fundamental levels. In countering this view, we offer several Prayer Principles outlining a biblical perspective on the nature and purpose of prayer.

Prayer Principle: Simply adding "in Jesus' name" does not guarantee a yes.

In John 15:7, Jesus says, "If you remain in me and my words remain in you, ask whatever you will, and it will be done for you." In verse 16 of the same chapter, the Lord says, "Whatever you ask the Father in My name, He may give you." Jesus repeats a similar promise in John 16:23–24. What are we to make of this claim? Based on these passages from John 15 and 16, we essentially have carte blanche in our prayer life. That is, we may confidently ask the Lord for just about anything, provided that our requests are in accord with His Word, His purposes, and that our petitions are for His glory. The qualification, "in My name," which Jesus adds in John 15:16, is presented within the context of a longer sermon that deals with God's great plans for history and humanity.

Everything Jesus ever said or did was about establishing the kingdom of God in the hearts of men. In the context of those verses, Jesus was preparing His disciples for the time after the resurrection when He was going to use them to establish His church upon which the gates of hell would not prevail (Matt 16:18). He told them they would do greater works than He did because He was going to the Father. When Jesus told His disciples that "whatever you ask the Father in My name, He will give you" (John 15:16), He wasn't giving them a magic formula as a means of using God to get healthy, wealthy, and wise. He was giving them His promise that if they asked Him for anything in His name *that might advance the kingdom of God*, He would provide what they needed.

Jesus is not saying, "If you pray for a new car and end the request with, 'In my name,' that He would promise to grant it" (although He may). What the promises in John 15 and 16 are claiming is that if our prayers are for God's glory, beneficial for Christ's Great Commission, and are motivated by a desire to see His kingdom advanced then, yes, we can pray "big" prayers and expect significant results.

Proponents of the prosperity gospel may counter with the argument that providing that new car, better job, or bigger house for them does advance the kingdom of God because "who would be attracted to a God who does not take care of His children?" Yet this assumes people are only attracted to God because they are searching for a heavenly benefactor. If this does happen to be the case, then one might question their love for God. God is more concerned about the prosperity of our souls than the prosperity of our bank accounts. If that were His priority, would He not have had the same prosperity for His only Son? Scripture tells us that while Jesus was engaged in His public ministry, He did not even have a place to lay His head—He was homeless (Matt 8:20).

James reminds us that the answer to our prayers is often denied because we pray with the wrong motives in mind. In Jas 4:3 we read, "You ask and don't receive because you ask with wrong motives, so that you may spend it on your evil desires." If your prayers are motivated by selfishness, then you should not expect God to say yes even if you present your request to Him with the proper tagline. However, God eagerly waits to hear from us whenever we ask for things that will advance the gospel message.

Prayer Principle: Your "amount of faith" has nothing to do with the answers to certain prayers.

Some ministers on TV assure their followers that God will do almost anything for them if only they "have enough faith." Is this really true? Are some things beyond our control, regardless of how much faith we have (or think we have)? The answer is *yes*. God already revealed His will and plan for certain things, and we may have absolute confidence that these things will be accomplished regardless of our prayers. His will must prevail.

This truth helps address the question of why God does not heal amputees by miraculously allowing lost limbs to regrow. We could offer other examples. For example, a person might have a facial scar from an accident, but the visible scar will remain even if the person accepts Christ. An alcoholic might become a Christian, and though his sins are now forgiven, he may still contract cirrhosis of the liver. Similarly, a veteran who lost a leg in war may become the most devout Christ follower ever, yet the missing limb will not grow back. No amount of faith and no amount of prayer, however earnest, could change these things. Why?

A recent scientific article addressed this question. The author, writing from an evolutionary perspective, wondered why some animals, such as starfish and salamanders, are able to regrow limbs, while humans cannot. The author speculated, "Does God Hate Amputees?" A couple of things are worth noting. First, human arms, hands, fingers, legs, feet, and toes are considerably more complex than the severed tail of a lizard or tentacle of a starfish. The complexity of a human appendage does not mean God could not restore it (after all, He made them in the first place), but the difference in classification is worth noting.[2]

Second, and more important, animals may have a body and a certain level of consciousness, but humans have a body and a soul that will live forever. God's primary work in the life of a believer, which He accomplishes to a large degree through prayer, is to redeem and sanctify the soul. God does not regrow severed limbs here on earth because a restored body is promised to all believers in the future. In the present, however, the primary mission of God is spiritual restoration. His focus for each of us, then, is the redemption of the soul and sanctification of the heart. Consequently, sincere prayers oriented toward this spiritual mission of God are answered in the affirmative and often with visible results.

We must also keep in mind that God has promised to heal every physical malady ever faced by any Christian when He gives each believer a new body in heaven (Rom 8:11, 23–25; 1 Cor 15:53–55; 2 Cor 5:1–8). Regarding the question of why God does not heal the amputee, the issue is really one of *timing*. God will restore the bodies of all amputees (born-again amputees, at least) in heaven. He has promised to do so. He has already made a way in which the amputee can get a new limb: become a Christian and enjoy a whole body once in heaven.

What are we to do then with the words of Jesus who told His disciples, "If you have faith the size of a mustard seed, you will tell this mountain, 'Move from here to there,' and it will move. Nothing will be impossible for you" (Matt 17:20)? First of all, as we look at the context of these verses, we see that His disciples had attempted unsuccessfully to cast a demon out of a young boy. They came to Jesus privately afterwards to ask why they had failed. Keep in mind that they had been given the same authority their Master had to cast out demons and heal the sick. Jesus cast out the demon and healed the boy, but afterward He rebuked His disciples for their *unbelief.* The problem was not that they did not have enough faith but that they did not have any faith at all in the matter. If your town was facing a serious drought and someone called a prayer meeting to pray for rain, would it not make sense to bring your raincoat with you to the prayer meeting?

Did Jesus mean that a believer could literally move a mountain with the tiniest speck of faith? No. It should be obvious to anyone that Jesus was speaking figuratively here. Jesus commonly used figurative language when He spoke to people just as we do today.

If I were to say to you, "It is raining cats and dogs outside," would you go outside and expect to see actual cats and dogs falling from the sky? Jesus was saying that even the most mountainous problems must be prayed for in faith if we expect to see God answer.

Prayer Principle: While you can, indeed, "pray about anything," remember that prayer was not given so that God could become our cosmic concierge.

Could you pray for a better parking spot? Sure. But why not get some exercise and leave the "good" parking spaces to bless someone else? Could we pray that our favorite restaurant has apple pie instead of coconut cream pie? Yes. But why not choose to eat at a restaurant that you know already serves apple pie? Do we really need to pray about something that is already within our own power to accomplish or obtain? One might ask, "Does not God care about every detail of our lives?" Sure He does. Do you think that when you stand before Him in heaven, He is going to say, "I wish you would have spent more time asking me for better parking spots and apple pie?" Before praying about the trivial things in your day (that tend to focus on "me" and "mine"), make sure you have *first* spent ample time in praying about how we can become more Christlike. Pray for God to protect Christians in Muslim countries facing persecution and martyrdom for the faith and that God will purge us of carnality so that we may be more like Jesus.

Someone might object, claiming they can talk to their heavenly Father about *anything*. I agree. We can pray to God about everything, even parking spots. Yet we ought to give equal time, if not more time, to prayers oriented toward the mission of God. God is not our "cosmic concierge." Many hotels employ concierges, whose job it is to get you anything you ask, and quickly, too. I have been helped by concierges on many occasions. They can call a cab for you. They can help you find your lost cell phone. They will tell you where the best pizza is in town and will lend you an umbrella to use as you walk there. Concierges are fine folks, but God is not one of them.

What we pray about speaks volumes about our spiritual maturity. As we mature in Christ, there will be less and less of "me" and more and more of "Him" in our prayers. D. L. Moody once wrote: "Prayer does not mean that I am to bring God down to my thoughts and my purposes, and bend His government according to my foolish, silly, and sometimes sinful notions. Prayer means that I am to be raised up . . . into union and design with Him; that I am to enter into His counsel and carry out His purpose fully."[3] The spiritually mature believer will pray with a mind-set that puts God's plan to usher in the kingdom first and has the ultimate goal of personal sanctification in mind so that they might become better used of God rather than becoming a better user of God.

Prayer Principle: The results of prayer are always a reflection of God's wisdom, power, and goodness.

One of the biggest mistakes people make when praying is to assume they know what is best for them. We do not possess perfect knowledge of the situation we are praying about, but God does. As stated in an earlier chapter, God sees the beginning from the end and the end from the beginning. He knows how a particular situation will turn out, and He knows what might come about if He granted the petition of a believer.

Luke 11:9–13 states,

> So I say to you, keep asking, and it will be given to you. Keep searching, and you will find. Keep knocking, and the door will be opened to you. For everyone who asks receives, and the one who searches finds, and to the one who knocks, the door will be opened. What father among you, if his son asks for a fish, will give him a snake instead of a fish? Or if he asks for an egg, will give him a scorpion? If you then, who are evil, know how to give good gifts to

your children, how much more will the heavenly Father give the Holy Spirit to those who ask Him?

Taken out of context, it would seem that Jesus is signing a blank check for believers to draw on heaven's bank account. That is not the case for several reasons. First, the gift that is being referred to here is the Holy Spirit. God answered that prayer for the disciples on the day of Pentecost, and He continues to give this gift to every believer since the day of Pentecost. If someone claims to be a believer but does not have the Holy Spirit dwelling in him, then he does not know God (Rom 8:9).

Second, Jesus compares His Father to a good earthly father who gives careful, paternal consideration to the things he gives to his children. He understands that the desires of his children must be weighed against all possible outcomes and consequences. So if granting the desires of our hearts will actually lead our hearts astray from following Him, would it be wiser for Him to give us what we want or what He knows is best? If answering no to our prayer leads us through troubled times, yet those troubled times help us trust Him more, would it be wiser for Him to give us what we want or what He knows is best? What if He simply has a better answer in mind? What we consider good may not be His very best for us. Would it be wiser to give us what we want or what He knows is best?

The 2003 comedy *Bruce Almighty* presents an interesting illustration. Jim Carey portrays a disgruntled TV reporter named Bruce. He can't seem to catch a break in life and rages against God. So God grants Bruce divine powers and challenges him to do a better job. Bruce begins to hear the prayers of people in his head. Eventually, he decides to have the prayers delivered to his e-mail. After typing furiously for a few minutes in reply to the requests, millions more show up in his e-mail inbox. In frustration he decides to simply answer yes to everything—which later results in mass chaos and disappointment.

Unlike Bruce, God certainly has the power to answer even our most difficult prayers. Yet we must understand that He also always exercises His power responsibly and informed by His omniscience. In light of His wisdom and knowledge of all things, answering yes to many of our prayers may be the most unloving thing He could do.

Should a concerned Father want to alleviate the suffering of His children and make them more comfortable? Would any parent who had the power to intervene and heal the broken heart of his offspring want to do so without delay? Not if denying their request accomplished a deeper purpose. Joni Eareckson Tada, who became a paraplegic as a result of a diving accident at age seventeen, says God "[permits] what He hates, to accomplish something He loves."[4] In other words, sometimes God uses the fires of affliction to purge His children of impurities just as a refiner uses heat to remove the dross from silver. If He did not allow the heat of the fire to be raised, the result would be inferior, polluted, weakened silver, unworthy and incapable of being of service for the kingdom.

Paul wrote: "Therefore we do not give up. Even though our outer person is being destroyed, our inner person is being renewed day by day. For our momentary light affliction is producing for us an absolutely incomparable eternal weight of glory. So we do not focus on what is seen, but on what is unseen. For what is seen is temporary, but what is unseen is eternal" (2 Cor 4:16–18). Materialism says that suffering happens and a person can do nothing about it. You have to endure it. By contrast Christianity says that suffering serves to build a stronger relationship with our heavenly Father.

For every trial and tribulation a believer faces, God, out of His goodness, always supplies His children with His comforting presence. To the nation of Israel God promised, "When you pass through the waters, I will be with you; and through the rivers, they shall not overwhelm you; when you walk through fire you shall not be burned, and the flame shall not consume you" (Isa 43:2 ESV).

Notice, He did not say "*if* you pass through the waters" but "*when* you pass through the waters." Everyone will face difficult times. He did not promise to supply a boat to smoothly cross over, nor did He promise to extinguish the flames. He promised the best thing He could: to meet them there and *be with* them.

We know Jesus prayed three times in the garden of Gethsemane that if there was any way possible—any way that our sins might be paid for other than the cross—that God might take away the cup He was about to drink (Matt 26:36–44). The Father had answered every other petition His Son had ever made, but this one He could not. The path to the cross had already been laid out even before the foundation of the world. In Luke's account of this event, he records something the other Synoptic writers did not: "And there appeared to him an angel from heaven, strengthening him" (Luke 22:43 ESV). In His humanity Jesus was distressed over the ordeal He knew He faced over the next several hours. He needed strength for the task, and God provided that through the presence of this ministering angel. When the Son faced His moment of suffering, the Father met Him there with strength equal to the task that lay before Him. God has promised the same for His adopted sons and daughters.

Conclusion

Prayer can do anything God can do provided the thing we ask for is in accordance with His will and ultimate purpose for our lives. While we as believers are free to pray about anything, we ought to spend our precious time with God praying about the things that have eternal significance rather than about our worldly desires. When we spend our time and energy praying for kingdom matters, not only will it have an impact in deepening our personal relationship with God, but it will result in the spread of the gospel message and the upbuilding of the kingdom. Below is a chart summarizing the function and purpose of prayer noting what prayer *is* and *is not*.

What Is Prayer?	
Prayer IS:	**Prayer IS NOT:**
Dependent on God's wisdom	Contingent on our wishes
Primarily beneficial through bringing us closer to God	Primarily about getting things from God
God helping us better understand His person, power, and providence	Us helping God to be informed about our needs, wants, or situation
About people and history being shaped in light of divine purposes	About God acting (or changing His plans) in light of human situations
A relationship that fosters greater intimacy with God	A mere channel of communication necessary because of our dependency on God
A lifelong journey, an ever-deepening conversation that serves to heighten our trust in God	Sporadic pleas, issued as needed, with uncertainty as to how (or whether) God will respond

God's chief desire is to prosper our souls rather than our bank accounts. However, if He does choose to prosper our bank accounts, we know that it is not for our comfort but for the furtherance of the kingdom.

Endnotes

1. David Van Biema and Jeff Chu, "Does God Want You to Be Rich?" *Time* (September 18, 2006): 56.

2. Judith Lipton and David Barash, "Does God Hate Amputees?" http://www.psychologytoday.com/blog/pura-vida/201210/does-god -hate-amputees, accessed November 25, 2012.

3. Dwight L. Moody, *Prevailing Prayer: What Hinders It?* (Chicago: Fleming H Revell, 1884), 102.

4. Joni Eareckson Tada, *The God I Love: A Lifetime of Walking with Jesus* (Grand Rapids: Zondervan, 2003), 357.

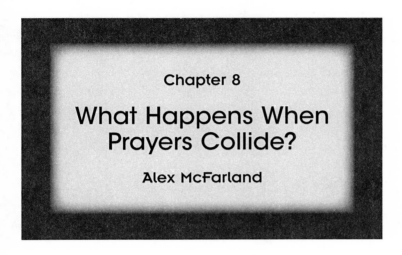

Chapter 8

What Happens When Prayers Collide?

Alex McFarland

S pending a rare Saturday off at a high-school soccer game is not exactly my favorite thing to do. Not long ago I did give up part of my weekend to attend a play-off game at the request of a close family friend. What made this game particularly interesting was that the opposing teams were both state champs in their divisions. Both teams had enjoyed statewide coverage in the local newspapers, and both teams featured starters who had been offered soccer scholarships at major universities once their high school careers were over. Though I would not consider myself an avid soccer fan, as hundreds of fans eagerly poured into the stands to watch the game, the excitement became contagious.

Both teams happened to be from Christian high schools. Moments before the match began, both teams grouped together for prayer at their respective ends of the field. The prayer huddles broke up, the teams high-fived one another, and the players assembled in the middle of the field to begin. About this time I heard someone remark, "Somebody's prayers are not going to get answered today!"

Assuming both teams prayed similar prayers—for a safe game, good sportsmanship, and a victorious outcome—clearly, both teams could not win. The game did go into multiple overtimes, and during the tense final moments as the score was tied, I watched many in the stands praying (probably parents, thinking about potential scholarship money that hung in the balance). The game was eventually settled in a "shoot out" (a new soccer term I learned that day).

I suppose everyone's prayers *were* answered that day; it is just that some of those intercessions received a no. Driving home I thought about the mutually exclusive requests rising up to heaven that day: *How often does God get prayer requests that conflict?* I wondered. Instantly, thoughts of opposing prayer requests and multiple possible answers and outcomes to a given prayer began to accumulate in my mind. I prayed a prayer of thanks to God that He, and not me, was responsible for figuring out the appropriate answers!

Counterpoint

What happens when two equally godly people are praying for opposite things? Is God conflicted on what to do when a farmer prays for rain to quench his fields while an avid soccer player in the same town prays for good weather so his soccer tournament will be held? Furthermore, can prayer counteract the free will of people or things about which we pray? What might God do when prayers collide? One possible way to resolve these problems is to appeal exclusively to God's sovereignty at the expense of human free will. In such cases human agency in prayer is diminished. Another response would be to moderate God's role by lessening His power, foreknowledge, or interest. In this case God's sovereignty is diminished. Both extremes, we will see, are biblically imbalanced.

Point

Like many of the questions we have already addressed, the tension inherent in the question of this chapter—what happens when prayers collide?—resides in the issue of a divine versus human perspective. Thus far we have posed the question from a purely human perspective. Yet the tension that exists becomes more manageable, though perhaps not completely resolved, once we view the circumstances from God's perspective (to the degree we are able). With this in mind, it could rightly be said that God's nature defines, at least to a degree, how He will respond to our prayers. This does not mean God is limited in any way. But in light of God's nature as defined by Scripture, some parameters logically define how our prayers will be handled. If our conclusions are shaped by these truths, we may have a reasonable degree of confidence in them. Several Prayer Principles follow, which seek to orient the reader to God's perspective on seemingly conflicting prayers.

Prayer Principle: God's answer to prayer is governed by His holiness and omniscience as He moves human history to its intended goal.

Most would agree that God's holiness and omniscience are key divine attributes (characteristics that are essential because of who He is). Because God is holy, He would not answer a prayer in a way that causes sin or promotes evil. Likewise, because God has all knowledge (i.e., omniscience), He could not mistakenly answer a prayer in a way that the repercussions later take Him by surprise. God has insights and knowledge beyond what we could possibly know (to say the least). David declared, "You know when I sit down and when I stand up; You understand my thoughts from far away. You observe my travels and my rest; You are aware of all my ways. Before a word is on my tongue, You know all about it, LORD" (Ps 139:2–4). There is nothing that we can say, think, or do that He does not already know. Jesus said that God knows the things we need before we even ask (Matt 6:8). God knows all about every possible circumstance, and He can foresee every possible repercussion of every possible turn a situation might take. Consequently, His holiness and omniscience govern the way He answers prayer.

Furthermore, God has an overarching plan for history that will come to pass. It stands to reason, then, that He would not implement an answer contrary to His prescribed course. Therefore, an answer to a prayer that we may, at the moment, find unsatisfactory might actually have prompted tears of joy had we only known all that God knows about "the big picture."

Prayer Principle: Whether in response to our prayer or by His free choice, God acts sovereignly, providentially, and redemptively.

Having established some of the more fundamental aspects of God's nature—holiness and omniscience—and the reality of His overarching plan for history, it is important to consider more narrowly how God acts as a reflection of His nature and plan. First, God's priorities do not conflict (though people's priorities often may). God's most pressing priority is fulfilling His plan of redemption; therefore, the assumption would be that any prayer that led to the salvation of lost people or the sanctification of a saint would be the prayer He would answer first.

Second, God's words do not conflict (though our understandings of them may). Things we pray for that might be in contradiction to God's Word will only be answered in light of God's Word. Suppose a woman leaves her husband simply because she is no longer happy with their relationship and moves in with another man who *is* making her happy. If she prayed and asked God to bless her new relationship, would He do so in light of the fact that she is living in adultery and does not have a scripturally valid reason for divorce? The woman feels that God wants her to be happy, but God is more concerned for her holiness.

Third, God's answering of our prayers is guaranteed to be perfect (though our asking is not). The Bible says that we don't really know what we ought to be praying for (Rom 8:26). The Holy Spirit, therefore, makes intercession for us (prays on our behalf). God knows what we need even before we ask (Matt 6:8), but oftentimes we humans simply do not know what we ought to pray for.

Prayer Principle: In cases where prayers seem to collide, God will answer in a way that is logically meaningful.

In light of this last principle, we can assume that God will answer prayer in a way that is logically meaningful. Because I interact with many professed atheists, let me say a word about what I mean by "logically meaningful" prayers. Periodically (several times per month) I get e-mails from a wiseacre who asks if God would answer a prayer for "a one-ended stick." Or will God make "two identical twins, yet each one taller than the other?" Such sarcastic attempts to put God to the test say more about the heart of the questioner than about the power of God. God is under no obligation to perform parlor tricks or to break the laws of logic to placate a skeptic.

While some prayer requests are intentionally formulated illogically, some might *unintentionally* bring an illogical request to God. One lady asked me, "Why will God not reveal to us what He was doing before eternity?" She had prayed for insight about this, and I began to explain that since *eternity*, by definition, means "forever," even God could not have been doing something *before* forever. My point is that we may be confident God's answers will always be logically meaningful.

Our concern here, however, relates to prayers that would require *mutually exclusive* answers. With seven billion people plus walking the planet on any given day, I suppose this is possible. Yet because so many minute details are relevant to each of our lives (and therefore, intricately entwined in the way we relate to God), I do think this contradictory prayer conundrum happens more rarely than you might think. Let us assume that one person somewhere is asking God a specific request, and at the same time another person is asking God for the exact opposite thing. Two simple examples just for illustration purposes might be: prayers for a rainstorm to occur on a certain day in South Bend, Indiana, or not, or two teen boys, each praying for the same girl to say yes to their respective prom invitations. There are several logically meaningful ways the prayer answerer—God—might field multiple requests that necessitate differing answers.

First, God could ignore any or all of the conflicting prayer requests. Remember that God is under no compunction to answer any prayers at all. Assuming that an actual dilemma of contradictory prayers is presented, God could resolve this by not answering at all. He could exercise providential prerogative, and this would not compromise His nature or His Word.

Second, God could say no to both parties and do something completely different. The girl jilts both of the boys who invited her to the prom and instead attends the prom with a third boy whom *she* asked. Or she does not go at all. In essence God is saying no to both boys' requests, and He would not be unjust to do so.

Third, God could say yes to both parties without committing a logical contradiction. Let's say an avid soccer player prays that no precipitation causes the tournament game to be canceled, while a local farmer urgently asks for rain that will save his corn crop. God could send rain to the farmer's fields while keeping it sunny in the uptown area where the game is taking place.

Fourth, God could give each party something different from what they had asked for (yet better). Consider a job seeker who is fervently praying for a job with company A. However, his wife secretly prays that he gets a job with company B because she does not like the thought of having to move to the city where company A is located. What if God answers by providing a job with company C that offers better benefits and a larger salary without the need for relocation? They both received their primary request—a new job—but with better perks.

Prayer Principle: God does not necessarily have to change a person's free will in order to answer our prayers in the areas where another's free will is involved.

Free will has been a contentious issue in Christian circles, but it seems to me that God has created us with the ability to choose our own actions—even if those actions lead to dreadful consequences for us or others. C. S. Lewis writes:

> Some people think they can imagine a creature which was free but had no possibility of going wrong; I cannot. If a thing is free to be good, it is also free to be bad. And free will is what has made evil possible. Why, then, did God give them free will? Because free will, though it makes evil possible, is also the only thing that makes possible any love or goodness or joy worth having.[1]

Another question to consider, then, is, Could our prayers override the free will of another person? We often pray about things that will, it seems, only be answered if God overrides the free will of another person. What if you, as a believer, were traveling to another country that was closed to the gospel? You arrive at the airport knowing that you are bringing Bibles in your suitcase to give away and that they could possibly be confiscated if they were discovered by customs agents. So you pray that the Lord might keep the agent from searching your luggage. Is that asking God to override the free will of the agent? What if a friend wanted to have an abortion and you fervently prayed that God might change her mind? Are you asking God to supersede her will? What if you were praying that God might move in the hardened heart of a loved one so that he might come to Christ? Are you asking God to change his or her free will?

God might answer these prayers in a way that does not interfere with anyone's free will. God could cause a distraction for the customs agent at just the right moment—say someone called him on his radio—and instead of searching your luggage, he simply waves you on through the checkpoint. God could answer the prayer for your friend who was considering the abortion by burdening a caring Christian to go to the abortion clinic where she meets your friend on the sidewalk outside and presents her with acceptable alternatives to abortion. The pregnant woman then chooses the alternative. What if your prayers for the salvation of that hard-hearted loved one moved God to send a trial into his life which finally brings him to his knees in repentance after realizing that God is his only answer?

So when we offer prayers that would seem to require God to override the free will of the person for whom we are praying, God could answer in a way that does not require Him to violate their own free will. He is powerful enough to orchestrate circumstances and events or prompt others to take actions that will accomplish the request of the intercessor and still leave the person free to choose their actions.

Let us also consider the possibility that God works in the heart of a person to change his or her mind about a particular issue. Is that the same as interfering in the person's free will? In the case of the customs agent—these agents are trained to look for people engaged in suspicious activities (it's called profiling). God could grant you favor with the customs agent so that he changes his mind about searching your luggage. God influenced the agent's thinking, but he still made the choice to let you pass.

In the case of the woman seeking the abortion, what if, in a moment of doubt about her choice, she willfully sought out alternatives to the abortion because her friend prayed and God placed that doubt in her mind about the decision? She still had the free will to ignore her doubts and go through with the procedure, but faced with the new information—that there were alternatives—she chooses not to abort her child.

In the case of the unbelieving relative, what if God—after years of drawing this man to Himself—simply moved in the heart of this man one more time, opening his spiritual eyes and ears, causing him to be more receptive to the gospel? In that moment of conviction, he could still say no but instead says yes to Jesus. God responded to the prayer for his salvation by influencing his thinking regarding sin and salvation without changing the unbeliever's will.

Through our willingness to listen to His voice, God may influence our way of thinking about a particular situation or choice that we are inclined to make. This influence in no way interferes with our free will because we are still free to resist His influence. We might pray for God to work in someone's heart, to cause them to change, but ultimately they don't have to change.

God may even resort to more drastic measures to change our way of thinking and make us willing to choose His way instead of our way. Consider the case of the prophet Jonah. God called him to go and preach to the Ninevites—a people that he and the Israelites hated (with good cause). They were wicked people and according to some of their own writings were known to flay their enemies alive among other dreadful things. Jonah refused to heed God's call to go and preach repentance to the people in Nineveh; instead, he fled to Tarshish aboard a ship.

It was not exactly a pleasure cruise for Jonah or his unfortunate shipmates. Scripture says, "Then the LORD hurled a violent wind on the sea, and such a violent storm arose on the sea that the ship threatened to break apart" (Jonah 1:4). The men on that ship began to cry out to their gods for deliverance. The captain then discovered the wayward prophet sleeping in the lower part of the ship. He woke Jonah and told him to call out to his God for help. The men then cast lots to determine who had sinned and brought this awful fate upon them. The lot fell on Jonah, and his secret was now going to be revealed. Jonah told the men he was running away from God and that they should throw him overboard so the storm would cease. Eventually, when they could see no other way, they threw Jonah overboard into the storm-tossed sea. The storm ceased, and the men called on the God of Jonah.

Apparently this demonstration of God's pursuing power was not going to be enough to grab Jonah's attention. The Bible says, "Now the LORD had appointed a huge fish to swallow Jonah, and Jonah was in the fish three days and three nights" (Jonah 1:17). From God's perspective this fish was a divinely designed instrument of deliverance. From the belly of the fish, Jonah decided that running from God was not a wise option, and he repented of his disobedience. God then commanded the fish to vomit Jonah out onto the shore. He called to Jonah a second time, and Jonah obeyed.

Could Jonah have made a different choice? Absolutely! If Jonah had chosen differently, God could have raised up another prophet to send to Nineveh to preach His message. Ultimately, God's plans will be fulfilled in this world whether we choose to be a part of them or not. By His grace God invites us to join His work, and we get to decide if we are going to participate.

Ultimately, God *could* interfere with the free will of those He created—if He decided to. This would seem logical since He created their minds, their personalities, their emotions, and their intellect. However, He chooses not to interfere because to do so, He would have to revoke our freedom to choose. When we freely choose to obey Him, to surrender to Him, and to follow His will, He delights in that choice. However, we must be free to choose the opposite in order to be genuine in our decisions. He does not coerce us to love Him, for a coerced love would not be genuine. God does not necessarily have to change a person's free will in order to answer our prayers in the areas where others' free will is involved.

Conclusion

Back in the early nineties, country music artist Garth Brooks recorded the chart-topping hit "Unanswered Prayers." In the song Brooks told about meeting an old high-school flame and introducing her to his wife. He remembered how he had prayed that this woman would become his wife. The song concludes with these lyrics:

> And as she walked away, and I looked at my wife
> And then and there I thanked the good Lord for the
>   gifts in my life.
> Sometimes I thank God for unanswered prayers
> Remember when you're talkin' to the Man upstairs
> That just because He may not answer, doesn't mean He
>   don't care.
> Some of God's greatest gifts are unanswered prayers.[2]

This song reflects the clarity one often has looking back at the sovereign hand of God in circumstances we originally had hoped, and even earnestly prayed, would turn out differently. Yet things are a bit more complex on this side of the circumstance. What we have endeavored to do in this chapter is offer the reader a glimpse into God's perspective. We have shaped this perspective around God's attributes as defined by Scripture. We conclude with a brief summary of one of the more salient Prayer Principles in the chart on the following page. Remembering that in His answers to prayer God acts sovereignly, providentially, and redemptively will help situate any circumstance within the "big picture."

God's answers to prayer are carried out in light of His:

Sovereignty	***Freedom and Justice*** No one forces God's hand; He will act righteously and cannot be coerced.
Providence	***Superintendence and Purpose*** God rules and "overrules"; He is neither arbitrary nor absent. The world therefore has direction and meaning.
Redemption	***Beneficence and Mercy*** God acts restoratively in nature and redemptively in people. His actions are full of grace, despite any appearances to the contrary. He always has a morally sufficient reason for what He does or allows.

Endnotes

1. C. S. Lewis, *Mere Christianity* (New York: Simon & Schuster, 1996), 52–53.

2. Patrick Alger, Garth Brooks, Larry B. Bastian, "Unanswered Prayers," Universal Music Publishing Group, 1990.

Chapter 9

Can Prayer Do Any Good in a World That Has Gone Bad?

Alex McFarland

A well-known Christian radio host was in the final moments of a Monday afternoon broadcast in November 2012. As always, a huge listening audience throughout Southern California had tuned in to hear the esteemed commentator's words. In this particular show the host, reflecting his Christian beliefs, remarked that if he were to die on the highway while headed home that night, he would go to heaven and live with God forever.

He could not have known how prophetic his words would turn out to be. Three hours later KKLA's Frank Pastore would be lying in the freeway, severely injured and comatose. An out-of-control motorist had run into Pastore, who was riding home from the studio on his motorcycle. At the time of this writing, Pastore was still in a coma at the medical center to which he had been airlifted.

Pastore was a "man's man," a former pro baseball player, Harley rider turned outspoken Christian leader. As a broadcaster Pastore had developed into an insightful, articulate voice for Christianity, often standing up for biblical teachings whether it was popular or not. Believers and nonbelievers alike respected the content of his *Frank Pastore Show*. In the aftermath of the wreck, many wondered, *How could God have let this happen? Why did God not protect such a choice Christian leader?*

In this chapter we will seek to establish the meaningfulness of prayer in the midst of suffering. First, we will briefly consider underlying assumptions that drive the view that human suffering necessarily implies that prayer is meaningless. Second, we will consider how suffering might actually serve the purposes of God and offer a few Prayer Principles that describe the role of prayer in the midst of suffering.

Counterpoint

The questions have echoed through the hearts of people and through centuries of time: Why God, why? If God can really act in the world (perform miracles), why is there so much evil? Why did God not stop something like the Holocaust? If God could have stopped the terrorists from killing innocent bystanders, and if any of the victims had been prayed for by their loved ones, then why did God not stop the terrorists? Such tragedies have caused many to question whether God is *able* to act in the world or *desires* to act in the world. The former calls into question God's greatness while the latter calls into question His goodness. If God is incapable of acting or unwilling to act, then the obvious implication is that prayer is meaningless.

Point

Before we can address the role and meaningfulness of prayer in the midst of suffering, it is important to reconcile the reality of suffering in a world controlled by God. Scripture does not seek to conceal the reality of suffering. On the contrary, it describes for the reader its origin, its divine purposes, and God's ultimate plan to remedy it. In what follows are several Prayer Principles describing this biblical trajectory and how prayer remains meaningful despite a world full of suffering.

Prayer Principle: Evil and suffering have their origins in human free will, and God's delay in eliminating them is a reflection of His mercy and patience toward sinners.

When God created the world, He created it good. There was no disease or death. No pain or suffering. No natural disasters. But when Adam and Eve made the choice to disobey God at the very beginning in the garden of Eden, all of creation was affected. Romans 8:20–21 says, "For the creation was subjected to futility—not willingly, but because of Him who subjected it—in the hope that the creation itself will also be set free from the bondage of corruption into the glorious freedom of God's children." We live in a fallen world. Disease, death, pain, suffering, and disasters are part of this fallen world. To eliminate all pain and suffering in our world, God would have to wipe the slate clean and start all over again. Eventually, He will redeem creation and restore the earth to its original state according to the promises in His Word.

God has given all humans free will. We are allowed to choose our own actions. He is not some holy puppeteer controlling our every motion. We have that control over our lives. Because of this, much of the suffering we experience in this life stems from the sinful actions of fallen people. God has given us a wonderful and awful gift in giving human beings free will. It is wonderful in the fact that we can make choices that result in good. It is awful in the fact that we may also choose to do evil—which has consequences. Regardless of the amount of good we do, we are still capable of choosing evil because we are sinful beings. Because sin has consequences, when we choose evil, those consequences affect not only us but innocent bystanders as well.

This reality is no more evident than in the example of the thousands of innocent people who were killed by terrorists' actions on September 11, 2001. Could God have stopped those planes from slamming into the World Trade Center and Pentagon and the field in Pennsylvania? Yes, but the terrorists had the free will to make choices. Innocent lives were lost, and untold suffering was caused because of their choices.

If God were to wipe out all evil and injustice, He would have to wipe out everyone. So it is not a question of God's ability to end the injustices and evils—because He could—but it is a question of His mercy toward sinners that stays His hand. Peter reminds us, "The Lord does not delay His promise, as some understand delay, but is patient with you, not wanting any to perish but all to come to repentance" (2 Pet 3:9). In other words, God's desire is to see people repent.

Before we hastily decide the matter is closed, we should consider whether we are asking the right question so that we might avoid jumping to the wrong conclusion. So the better question would be, Can God do something greater in the lives of people by allowing suffering to enter into their experience? In other words, could God have a morally sufficient reason for allowing suffering?

Prayer Principle: The reality of pain and suffering in the present serves God's purposes in the lives of His children.

You may have asked yourself: "If God is in control, why is there so much pain and suffering? Could God—the all-powerful One—perform a miracle and instantly wipe out the injustices and evils present in this world?" The simple answer is yes, He could, but He chooses not to for several reasons. Matthew 5:45 contains the famous phrase, "He . . . sends rain on the just and the unjust" (NKJV). Even godly people experience tragedies. Why is this, when many of them had fervently prayed for a different outcome? Why does pain remain in some lives, even after years of prayer for God's deliverance? Why have some of the most devout followers of Christ experienced a "thorn in the flesh"?

First, let us define "thorn in the flesh." This is one of those biblical phrases that has become so common in English speech that most would not know it was biblical at all. The phrase "thorn in the flesh" is an idiom (a common saying) which means "a constant nuisance." The image is of "a burr in the saddle." Think of a briar or thorn caught between a horse and a saddle, constantly cutting the skin with every movement of the rider. Sounds painful.

Paul talked about the things in his life that were persistently painful. In the second letter to the Corinthians he wrote:

> Therefore, so that I would not exalt myself, a thorn in the flesh was given to me, a messenger of Satan to torment me so I would not exalt myself. Concerning this, I pleaded with the Lord three times to take it away from me. But He said to me, "My grace is sufficient for you, for power is perfected in weakness." Therefore, I will most gladly boast all the more about my weaknesses, so that Christ's power may reside in me. So I take pleasure in weaknesses, insults, catastrophes, persecutions, and in pressures, because of Christ. For when I am weak, then I am strong. (2 Cor 12:7b–10)

Paul actually took joy in the fact that he had a thorn in the flesh. Why? Because the power and provision of the Lord was all the more clear in his life when persistent burdens forced him to lean fully on the Lord.

So the question becomes, could God have a good reason for allowing pain and trouble into our lives? In other words, might the "bad thing" that plagues your life be permitted because in time it will result in some "good things"? Consider the following six key reasons God allows pain and suffering to come into our lives.

First, God allows suffering to destroy sinful self-reliance, to purge us of self-sufficiency. The sinful nature of man compels him to live a life that is independent of God, and even after conversion there are times when he stubbornly tends to do his own thing. This independent streak has gotten man into trouble on more than one occasion—in fact, it got him evicted from paradise. When things are going our way, we tend to drift away from God—to forget that He is the One who meets our every need. God warned Israel never to forget that He had provided the prosperity that they would experience when He brought them into the Promised Land. "You may say to yourself, 'My power and my own ability have gained this wealth for me,' but remember that the LORD your God gives you the power to gain wealth, in order to confirm His covenant He swore to your fathers, as it is today" (Deut 8:17–18). Sometimes it takes the pain and suffering of our choices to make us realize we are utterly dependent on Him. C. S. Lewis wrote, "The creature's illusion of self-sufficiency must, for the creature's sake, be shattered."[1]

Second, God allows suffering to draw us back into His will. When we make choices that take us outside of God's revealed will for our lives, God gently nudges us to call us back to Him. He beckons and calls. Then, perhaps through some rather severe circumstances, we finally "get it," and we come back to Him. We need to fall on our knees before God. God will never override our free will; God does not force Himself on us. Children may think they are capable of crossing a busy street without help from their parents. Similarly, we may not think we need God every step of the way down the crossing of life. God knows we need Him! Pain can be a wake-up call that reminds us we need God. C. S. Lewis made reference to this in his book *The Problem of Pain*. Lewis wrote: "God whispers to us in our pleasures, speaks in our conscience, but shouts in our pain." Lewis went on to say, "Pain is God's megaphone to rouse a deaf world."[2]

Third, God allows suffering to build our character. Have you ever polished silverware? You are taking off the oxidized layer of dead material on the surface. The process reveals the pure metal underneath. If we allow God to have His way in our lives, pain can polish us, too. In Rom 5:3–5 we read, "We also rejoice in our afflictions, because we know that affliction produces endurance,

endurance produces proven character, and proven character produces hope. This hope will not disappoint us, because God's love has been poured out in our hearts through the Holy Spirit who was given to us." Suffering produces something; it changes us. Since the goal of the Christian life is to become more like Christ, we should see suffering as the polishing compound God uses to help produce Christlikeness in us.

Fourth, God allows suffering to teach us more about Him. Some things about God's faithfulness you might not learn any other way. Job was a righteous man who feared God and shunned evil. His faith was put to the test after Satan questioned his integrity before God. Satan contended that Job only remained faithful to Jehovah because of God's protection and provision. God knew otherwise. So Satan was given permission by God to attack Job's wealth, family, and health to prove Job's faithfulness (see Job 1–2). In spite of the horrendous suffering Job experienced, Scripture says, "Throughout all this Job did not sin in what he said." After a rather lengthy dialogue between Job and the friends who came to offer Job their counsel, God spoke to Job to remind him just how utterly insufficient Job was in light of the all-sufficiency of God. Job, after being admonished by God said, "I had heard rumors about You, but now my eyes have seen You. Therefore I take back my words and repent in dust and ashes" (Job 42:5–6). Job had learned more about God through his anguish and pain than he ever did through his prosperity.

Fifth, God allows suffering to validate our discipleship. In Heb 12:6–11 we read,

"For the Lord disciplines the one he loves, and chastises every son whom he receives." It is for discipline that you have to endure. God is treating you as sons. For what son is there whom his father does not discipline? If you are left without discipline, in which all have participated, then you are illegitimate children and not sons. Besides this, we have had earthly fathers who disciplined us and we respected them. Shall we not much more be subject to the Father of spirits and live? For they disciplined us for a short time as it seemed best to them, but he disciplines us for our good, that we may share his holiness. For the moment all discipline seems painful rather than pleasant, but later it yields the peaceful fruit of righteousness to those who have been trained by it. (Heb 12:6–11 ESV)

The writer here is speaking with some Christians, explaining that Christians suffer, and his own suffering proved that he was really one of God's own children. Parents discipline their children, not out of spite but in their best interest. A child that is not disciplined by parents is subject to bring disgrace on them. So we too, without discipline, could bring disgrace on our Father.

Sixth, God allows suffering to provide opportunities for worship, service, and reward. I have a friend who achieved his dream of playing football for the Dallas Cowboys, yet his NFL career was cut short by a life-threatening health issue. He nearly died, but several years of operations and therapy enabled him to survive. Today he speaks to groups about surviving a near-terminal illness, and his story gives hope to many people. Pain can pave the way for future opportunities for worship, service, and reward. Your thorn may be permitted in order to prepare you for some future ministry. Consider 2 Cor 1:3–4: "Praise the God and Father of our Lord Jesus Christ, the Father of mercies and the God of all comfort. He comforts us in all our affliction, so that we may be able to comfort those who are in any kind of affliction, through the comfort we ourselves receive from God." Comforting people who have experienced tragedy is much easier coming from those who have experienced the pain themselves. Sometimes God allows pain and suffering in the world to create spiritual opportunity.

Prayer Principle: Prayers are meaningful because in the midst of suffering and pain, God works to change the hearts of His children even if their circumstances do not change.

Some friends in ministry had a miscarriage back in January 2006. They went to the obstetrician for a routine sonogram only to discover that their child had died as a result of a neural tube defect. On top of that tragic event, on the day of the memorial service for their child, the husband's mother had a major heart attack that nearly took her home to heaven. She spent weeks in the hospital and rehabilitation but eventually made a limited recovery.

The rapid succession of events was disconcerting for them, and in the days following they pleaded with God to help them find meaning in the midst of their pain. Their prayers did not change their situation, but they eventually worked to change their own hearts. One thing they learned in the midst of their struggle was that while it is perfectly fine to ask God a question, it is never OK to question God. Eventually, through prayer they came to understand that God did not "take their child" but that the child's defect, which led to the miscarriage, was a result of living in a world plagued by the after-effects of the fall. Eventually God would use the situation in their ministry.

Several months later they were ministering at the Dallas Life Foundation—a homeless shelter operated by First Baptist Church in Dallas, Texas. As my friend was preaching a message from Acts 16 about Paul and Silas being imprisoned, he related the story of that trial to a chapel filled with men and women. After the message was over, several women in the shelter approached his wife and requested prayer. They too had been through miscarriages and were having a difficult time recovering from their tragedies. My friends' experience enabled them to comfort others who were dealing with the same pain. These women wanted to make sense of it all and found a kindred spirit who had been through what they had been through. Even in the midst of the disappointment and pain, my friends did not stop praying because through their prayers, they gained insight into God's purposes, and the testing produced character. Without prayer they would have lost hope.

Ravi Zacharias writes:

> Only so much about life can be understood by reason; so much falls far short of any reasonable explanation. Prayer then becomes the irrepressible cry of the heart at the times we most need it. For every person who feels that prayer has not "worked" for them and has therefore abandoned God, there is someone else for whom prayer remains a vital part of her life, sustaining her even when her prayers have gone unanswered, because her belief and trust is not only in the power of prayer but in the character and wisdom of God.[3]

We may not fully understand the why of our pain and suffering in this life, but we continue to cry out to God who gives us comfort and wisdom because our hearts long to find meaning. God is trustworthy. He may give us that insight as He did for the apostle Paul and for my friends who went through the pain of miscarriage, but He may choose to keep His reason veiled until we arrive safely on the shores of heaven. Christians can know that regardless of the reason for their suffering, "all things work together for the good of those who love God: those who are called according to His purpose" (Rom 8:28) and nothing can separate them from the love of God through Christ.

Again we must remember that we pray to God as part of our relationship with Him and not just to get what we want. When we connect with Him through prayer, we connect with the One who understands the suffering we experience in this life because, after all, He stepped down from His holy position in heaven to be born here on this earth and to walk among us. Jesus experienced isolation, sadness, hunger, thirst, exhaustion, loss, persecution, betrayal, injustice and was condemned to death on trumped-up charges. The Bible tells us that all this was necessary:

> Therefore, He had to be like His brothers in every way, so that He could become a merciful and faithful high priest in service to God, to make propitiation for the sins of the people. For since He Himself was tested and has suffered, He is able to help those who are tested. (Heb 2:17–18)

> For we do not have a high priest who is unable to sympathize with our weaknesses, but One who has been tested in every way as we are, yet without sin. Therefore let us approach the throne of grace with boldness, so that we may receive mercy and find grace to help us at the proper time. (Heb 4:15–16)

Conclusion

God permits struggles to enter our lives in order to purge us, call us, grow us, authenticate us, instruct us, and offer opportunities for service to us. The conclusions should not be, "God is evil," or "God is not powerful enough to fix the world." Equally erroneous would be the assumption (as Eastern religions teach) that what we think is morally evil or personally painful is mere illusion. Pain is real. Tell the parents of a dying child that their little one's cancer is due to "bad karma" or a lack of "enlightenment." They would not feel comforted. Tragedies occur, even to those we would call "good" people. Let's face it: we live in a broken world. Yet evil will not have the last word. Believers can trust that their pain and suffering are not arbitrary. They serve God's purposes until the time He chooses, in His power and goodness, to eradicate evil and restore His creation.

Endnotes

1. C. S. Lewis, *The Problem of Pain* (London: Geoffrey Bles, 1940), 85.

2. Ibid.

3. Ravi Zacharias, *Has Christianity Failed You?* (Grand Rapids: Zondervan, 2010), 144.

Chapter 10

Can Prayer Connect with a God Who Seems Hidden?

Alex McFarland

It was not much of a place to lay his head, but at least it gave him shelter from the elements. As he sat down at the entrance to the cave, all he could think about was how tired he was and how utterly disappointed and alone he felt. He had just spent forty long and quiet days trudging through the wilderness. In those moments of silence, he had to wonder, *Has God forgotten all about me? Am I really the only one left?* After all, he was not used to the silence, and the heavens were completely shut to him.

The memories of the recent victory on Mount Carmel were but a faint recollection for Elijah. He had seen the fire of God fall from the heavens, consuming the wet sacrifice he had prepared, thus silencing the prophets of Baal. The only thing he could think about was the words of Ahab's wife, Jezebel, who threatened to do to him what Elijah had done to the losers of that holy contest. Fear for his life had driven him to flee from her, and fear had led him to that secluded place where he could indulge in his self-pity.

As Elijah sat in the dark, cramped cave, the Lord broke the silence with a simple question, "What are you doing here, Elijah?" Instead of answering directly, Elijah registered his complaint. The prophet grumbled that he had faithfully fulfilled God's call, and yet he felt like a failure—as if he was the only one of the faithful left. The Lord then told him to go and stand on the mountain, in the presence of the Lord.

> At that moment, the LORD passed by. A great and mighty wind was tearing at the mountains and was shattering cliffs before the LORD, but the LORD was not in the wind. After the wind there was an earthquake, but the LORD was not in the earthquake. After the earthquake there was a fire, but the LORD was not in the fire. And after the fire there was a voice, a soft whisper. (1 Kgs 19:11–12)

The Lord had once again spoken to His servant, not in some big booming voice from the sky but in a soft gentle whisper, calling him back to the work God wanted this man to complete.

Like Elijah, believers at times experience moments in their lives when God is silent and His presence seems distant. They may have prayed about some difficult situation but heard nothing back from above. Perhaps God did not answer their prayers in a timely manner which brought about undesirable consequences. This "silent treatment" can become disturbing, leading one to wonder if God has turned a deaf ear to us or if we have done something to cause Him to stop loving us. Can our prayers connect to God even when He seems to be hidden from us? Does the silence mean we have been forsaken by Him? In this chapter we will explore the question of how Christian prayer connects with a God who, at times, seems silent. After addressing a few flawed assumptions on the topic, we will offer several biblically based Prayer Principles to help guide the reader through times of divine hiddenness.

Counterpoint

When God is silent, or He seems hidden, believers may be tempted to draw several unwarranted conclusions. In times of prolonged silence, for example, one may actually begin to deny God's existence. This is perhaps the most radical response to such circumstances. More common, however, might be the notion that God simply does not care, that one's prayers are inconsequential to a God who has much bigger problems to solve. Few would consider that God's silence might actually serve a larger purpose in the life of the believer. In what follows, we will explore the possibility that, far from suggesting God is absent or apathetic, God's perceived silence may be divinely intended for the good of the believer.

Point

Before we can address the question of how prayer connects with God when He seems hidden, it is important to understand what it means for God to speak to us as believers. Does it entail an audible voice from heaven or something mystical? After clearly establishing the character and means of God's revelation, we will then offer several Prayer Principles regarding the relationship between prayer and God's perceived hiddenness.

God has spoken to all of humanity in two primary ways. First, God speaks through *general revelation,* which is available to everyone, everywhere at all times. Romans 1:20 says, "For His invisible attributes, that is, His eternal power and divine nature, have been clearly seen since the creation of the world, being understood through what He has made. As a result, people are without excuse." There is enough general revelation through creation to prove that God exists. Sadly, some people have chosen to suppress the truth in their unrighteousness (Rom 1:18). If they deny the existence of God, then they assume they are not responsible to Him for their actions. According to Paul, this tendency to suppress the truth leads to idolatry (Rom 1:23, 25), deviant sexuality (Rom 1:24, 26–27), and other immoral behaviors (Rom 1:28–32).

One particular manifestation of general revelation is God speaking through the conscience by writing His laws on the heart of humanity. Paul wrote, "So, when Gentiles, who do not have the law, instinctively do what the law demands, they are a law to themselves even though they do not have the law. They show that the work of the law is written on their hearts. Their consciences confirm this. Their competing thoughts will either accuse or excuse them" (Rom 2:14–15). In other words, all people know instinctively what is right and wrong. The problem comes when they choose not to follow the dictates of their conscience.

Second, God also gave us *special revelation* through the Bible. While general revelation remains limited in scope, special revelation discloses all that God has chosen to make known about Himself and His plan to redeem us from the fall. Paul wrote, "All Scripture is breathed out by God and profitable for teaching, for reproof, for correction, and for training in righteousness, that the man of God may be complete, equipped for every good work" (2 Tim 3:16–17 ESV). When God speaks today, whatever He reveals to us will never contradict, replace, or add to His completed revelation, the written Word of God. If you "hear" Him telling you that it is OK to compromise in an area about which He has already clearly spoken in His Word, that voice is not from Him but from your own sinful desire.

The Bible further gives us record of God's special revelation to individuals through visions, theophanies (times when God manifested Himself physically), miracles, and, most importantly, the incarnation of Jesus Christ. Jesus, then, is God's ultimate special revelation to humanity. The writer to the Hebrews wrote:

> Long ago God spoke to the fathers by the prophets at different times and in different ways. In these last days, He has spoken to us by His Son. God has appointed Him heir of all things and made the universe through Him. The Son is the radiance of God's glory and the exact expression

of His nature, sustaining all things by His powerful word. After making purification for sins, He sat down at the right hand of the Majesty on high. (Heb 1:1–3)

In the original language, the phrase "the exact expression of His nature" conveys the image left in a piece of metal after it has been struck with an engraving tool and hammer. Christ is the exact image of the Father, and if anyone wants to know what the Father is like, they need to look at the Son.

Prayer Principle: While God can communicate to His children in many ways, the Holy Spirit is at the center of all God's communication.

While these details regarding the character and means of God's revelation are important, they still do not answer the question, Does God still speak today? We suggest that God does indeed continue to speak to His children. By definition Christianity is an intimate personal relationship with God rather than a religion. Dr. Henry Blackaby, author of *Experiencing God*, wrote that there are seven realities of experiencing God: "God speaks by the Holy Spirit through the Bible, prayer, circumstances, and the church to reveal Himself, His purposes, and His ways."[1] While God uses all of these methods to convey His will to His followers, at the center of all God's communication is the mediating role of the Holy Spirit.

The Holy Spirit speaks in several ways, though seldom through an audible voice. He convicts believers (and unbelievers) of sin, brings to mind Scripture, and prompts believers to take certain actions. There are a number of scriptural examples of this. In Acts 8, the Holy Spirit directed Philip to go down the road that goes from Jerusalem to Gaza where he met an Ethiopian man who was reading Scripture while riding in his chariot as he returned from Jerusalem. The Spirit prompted Philip to join this man and witness to him, and the man trusted Christ. In Acts 16 we read how Paul, while passing through Phrygia and Galatia, planned to take the gospel into Asia, but he was prevented from doing so by the Holy Spirit. So it is in the context of the Christian's daily walk that God communicates with believers as they read the Word, commune with Him in prayer, trust Him through their circumstances, and fellowship with other believers.

Prayer Principle: The apparent distance between the believer and God may be emotional or psychological, but it is not *actual*.

In reality, it is impossible for God to be distant. Psalm 139 talks about God's *omnipresence*, the fact that God is everywhere. Verse 8 (KJV) even points out that "if I make my bed in hell, . . . thou art there." If God is everywhere, ever present, and equally present throughout the universe, then He cannot really be distant from me. A number of Christian writers have expounded on the realization that although God may sometimes *seem* distant, it is impossible for Him actually to *be* distant. Max Lucado writes that in Jesus, God came near.[2] I would add that Jesus not only came near, but He *is* near! In response to the emptiness left in the aftermath of sin and in contrast to the despair that is ultimately promised by secularism, Christianity promises a Savior and Lord who, by His nature, is always present, always near. He *is*!

With this in mind, the believer can hold on to the reality of God's presence, even when He seems distant. God gave a wonderful promise to believers in Hebrews which says, "I will never leave you or forsake you" (Heb 13:5). Granted, this promise was given in the context of believers being content with what they have and not being lovers of money. Nevertheless, this promise applies to the total welfare of the believer. *The Believers Bible Commentary* says,

> The greatest riches a person can have lie in possessing Him who promises, "I will never leave you nor forsake you." In Greek, strong negation is expressed by using two or more negatives. (This is the opposite of English

structure in which a double negative makes a positive assertion.) In this verse the construction is very emphatic: it combines five negatives to indicate the impossibility of Christ deserting His own![3]

In spite of any emotional or psychological distress you might feel in the midst of your situation, God, based on His Word and His promises, will never abandon one of His children.

Prayer Point: The perception of God's distance may reflect a problem with the petitioner.

If God seems distant to us, maybe the issue is not with Him but with us. Ravi Zacharias writes, "I think the reason we sometimes have the false sense that God is so far away is because that is where we have put Him. We have kept Him at a distance, and then when we are in need and call on Him in prayer, we wonder where He is. He is exactly where we left Him."[4] Below are several potential problems one might consider when God seems distant.

First, the petitioner may not be a Christian. The most basic prayer is the prayer for salvation. You may not be going very far in your prayer life because you are not yet born again. Bear in mind that the prayer for salvation is not some magic formula or secret password that one can simply utter and gain entrance to heaven. It reflects a heart attitude that understands the severity of our situation as lost sinners before a holy God. Apart from Jesus Christ, we must bear the judgment for our own sins, which is eternity in hell. Balking at our predicament or complaining that God is unfair for prescribing such a dreadful punishment will not change the outcome. In fact, it indicates that we are entrenching deeper into our attitude of rebellion. There must be a conscious decision to repent of our sins, that is, to stop blindly pursuing sin and to start pursuing God. The "sinner's prayer" is only a verbal expression of this desire to exchange the old life of sin for a new life in Christ, which is only lived out with the help of the One who raised Jesus from the dead. If there has been no life change, no desire for holiness, and no concern for growing in Christ in your life, perhaps you need to take that all-important first step of repenting and believing the gospel.

Second, you may have unconfessed sin in your life. Psalm 66:18–19 (KJV) states, "If I regard iniquity in my heart, the Lord will not hear me: But verily God hath heard me; he hath attended to the voice of my prayer." Sometimes God seems distant to us because He wants us to be aware of some unconfessed sin we might be harboring in our hearts. The penalty of a believer's sin—eternal hell—has been satisfied at the cross by the blood of the sinless Son of God, but sin still hurts our fellowship with God. Suppose a child accidentally broke a window with his baseball and tried to hide the evidence from his father. When the father confronted the child about the incident, the child lied instead of admitting his error. Until that child owns up to the accident as well as the lie told to cover up the error, their relationship will be at an impasse. It is like that in our relationship with God. When we confess our sins to Him, He will restore our fellowship, remove that feeling of distance, and hear our prayers again.

In Psalm 32, King David reflects on a time when he had to own up to harboring sin in his life.

> When I kept silent, my bones became brittle from my groaning all day long. For day and night Your hand was heavy on me; my strength was drained as in the summer's heat. Selah. Then I acknowledged my sin to You and did not conceal my iniquity. I said, "I will confess my transgressions to the LORD," and You took away the guilt of my sin. Selah. (Ps 32:3–5)

If God seems distant to you, pray and ask Him to reveal any sin that you might be clinging to in your heart; that is one prayer God is more than willing to answer.

Third, the believer's heart may be full of unbelief. Jesus was unable to perform many miracles in His hometown because of the unbelief of the people there (Matt 13:58). When our hearts are filled with unbelief, God will not answer our prayers. Faith is the firm conviction that something is true and not just a blind hope that it's true. Do Christians have doubts sometimes? Absolutely! Whenever doubts enter, they provide a fertile seedbed for the weeds of unbelief to sprout and grow. An unbelieving heart will naturally feel distant from God because without faith, it is impossible to please God (Heb 11:6). How do we overcome those doubts? By remembering what God has done for us in the past! That is why God frequently reminded Israel that He had delivered them out of Egypt. Every time they looked at the Ten Commandments, they were reminded, "I am the LORD your God, who brought you out of the land of Egypt, out of the place of slavery" (Exod 20:2). If you find yourself feeling distant from God because you have allowed unbelief to grow in your heart, sit down with a piece of paper and write down some things God has done for you in the past. When you finish, pray and thank Him for those blessings.

Fourth, the believer might be relying too much on current circumstances to try to discern what God is saying. While God does speak through circumstances, the troubling situation we face today might make a complete turnaround tomorrow. Circumstances change but "Jesus Christ is the same yesterday, today and forever" (Heb 13:8). Also, we would do well to remember that this world is not the end-all and be-all of existence. This world is a laboratory for the formation of souls. It is a gymnasium for the perfecting of saints. As any top athlete will tell you, sometimes exercise hurts.

Fifth, believers might be misled by their emotions. Feelings are frequently mistaken. Emotions can steer you wrong about everything from romance to shopping. Studies show that most people choose the car they drive for emotional reasons. They leave the dealership having spent too much and often having committed themselves to a vehicle not exactly suited to their needs. If emotions cannot be fully trusted to handle the purchase of a consumer item, why would we trust emotions when it comes to an ultimate, soul-impacting topic like God? We are much better off trusting His revelation about reality than our possible misconceptions.

Today God may seem distant to you, but remember that there was a time when you were distant from Him. Before you became a Christian, was God's love for you less than it is now? Of course not! Thus, as a believer I can know that, despite our emotions, God's love for me is as constant as it ever was. We tend to think of ourselves as being "in God's favor" when things are going well and perhaps "out of favor" when life gets tough. Do not be misled into concluding that God's love has changed simply because you do not feel a level of bliss you once experienced in light of past circumstances. Remember, we do not worship feelings or circumstances. We are in a relationship with the God who *is* joy and with the sovereign Lord who is in control of all circumstances.

Sixth, it could be that God's sovereign timetable is just not the same as yours. Someone once said that God is not an "on-time God," but He is an "in-His-time God" meaning that God does not operate on the same timetable as we do. It would be a mistaken conclusion on our part to assume that God has abandoned us when we do not see our prayer answered in the time frame we think it ought to be answered. In our impatience we often jump to that conclusion, and our lack of patience can often cause us to push ahead of God.

At the age of seventy-five, Abraham was given the promise that God would make from him a great nation and that his descendants would inherit Canaan even though he had no male heir at the time (Gen 12:1–4). After about ten years of living in Canaan, Abraham's wife Sarah began to lose patience with the Lord and proposed that Abraham take Hagar, her handmaiden, as a surrogate mother to start this family. Abraham agreed. When Hagar conceived and had a child, Sarah became jealous and began to blame Abraham and persecute Hagar (Gen 16:1–6). In their impatience they took matters into their own hands and created many more problems than they solved. At the age of 100, Abraham finally received the promised son, Isaac, through whom God fulfilled His promise (Gen 21:5). God fulfilled the promise according to His timetable and not Abraham's. Commenting on Psalm 130, Charles H. Spurgeon says,

> If the Lord Jehovah makes us wait, let us do so with our whole hearts; for blessed are all they that wait for Him. He is worth waiting for. The waiting itself is beneficial to us: it tries faith, exercises patience, trains submission, and endears the blessing when it comes. The Lord's people have always been a waiting people.[5]

Seventh, perhaps the believer has simply failed to notice God's work. It could be that God is listening, answering, and working in my life significantly, but I have been too busy to notice or thank Him for it. We may not see the direct answer to our prayers when we expect it, but we can measure the indirect results of our prayer and know that God is active. Character is shaped, faith is tested, trust is learned, and our witness is elevated before an unbelieving world when we patiently endure the silence. Too often we lean on feelings (which vacillate up and down, run hot and cold), and God wants us to lean on the fact of His Word (which never changes). We long for the spiritual high we felt after a move of God during revival or a retreat, and when that rush of excitement fades, there is nothing deep rooted to hold up our faith until the next mountaintop. This is why Paul prescribed prayer as the remedy for an anxious heart. He wrote, "Don't worry about anything, but in everything, through prayer and petition with thanksgiving, let your requests be made known to God. And the peace of God, which surpasses every thought, will guard your hearts and minds in Christ Jesus" (Phil 4:6–7). Faith has been likened to a train. Our faith is the engine which carries the load; God's promises are the boxcars (the facts), and our feelings always bring up the rear of the train as the caboose.

Prayer Principle: Every believer experiences times when God seems distant.

God's silence, however, need not necessarily reflect a problem with the petitioner. A quick examination of Scripture reveals that silence from God is not an unusual thing. In Gen 1:2, we read, "Now the earth was formless and empty, darkness covered the surface of the watery depths, and the Spirit of God was hovering over the surface of the waters." There was silence. After the passing of Joseph at the end of the book of Genesis, the Egyptians began to oppress the children of Israel and enslaved them. God had promised to bring the nation back into the land that had been promised to Abraham's descendants, yet it took 430 years for their deliverance from Egypt to come. We have nothing of the activity of God recorded in the canon of Scripture about that time of waiting. Silence. Between the closing of the Old Testament and the first advent of Christ (a time referred to as the intertestamental period), we have around 400 years of silence. History did not stop, but God's recorded revelation did. Even today, the canon of Scripture is closed, and no new revelation is being given to man by God. God has said all that needs to be said in His Word.

That being said, this explanation does not account for the times in our personal relationship with God when we feel that God is no longer near to us. After all, God did promise us His presence through the indwelling Holy Spirit. Paul referred to this promised indwelling as a "down payment in our hearts" until the day we are redeemed (2 Cor 1:22). So a believer might ask, "If God's Spirit dwells within me, why do I not feel Him right now? Have I done something to cause the Spirit to leave me?"

Prayer Principle: God's silence does not mean He is inactive, for His greatest work in your life may be accomplished during times of waiting.

If you are facing one of those times when God seems hidden and silent, it is important not to become angry, fearful, disappointed, or confused. God can use the silence as a tool to mold and shape you to be more Christlike and to build your confidence in His sovereignty. Below are several ways God could be using His silence for the benefit of the believer.

First, divine silence could be an opportunity for growth. When Jesus received news that Lazarus had died, He allowed two extra days to pass before He went to Bethany where He would raise Lazarus from the dead. As He approached the tomb, Martha confronted Jesus saying, "Lord, if You had been here, my brother wouldn't have died" (John 11:21). Her words were filled with disappointment; she felt abandoned in her hour of greatest need. When Jesus came to the tomb and saw all the mourners crying, He also began to weep, not because Lazarus had died but because of the unbelief of the crowd. Jesus then commanded Lazarus to come forth from the tomb, and Lazarus promptly obeyed. Would their faith in God have been strengthened had Jesus been there to prevent the death of Lazarus? Possibly. But which scenario increased their faith more, seeing Jesus heal the sick, which He did on numerous occasions, or seeing Him raise a man from the dead? Jesus said, "This sickness will not end in death but is for the glory of God, *so that the Son of God may be glorified through it*" (John 11:4, emphasis added). The waiting allowed them to learn something new about Jesus, namely that He had power over the greatest enemy of all—death. You too can learn something during the silence if you will listen.

Second, divine silence could be a teaching opportunity. So the job in Cincinnati did not come through, even though I really prayed for it. The candidate I voted for did not win the election, in spite of the fact that several in our study group fasted and prayed. Maybe God is not listening. Or maybe He is trying to get a point across to me. One of the greatest lessons a believer can learn from prayer is that deeper trust in God is better developed in the dark than in the light; in the silence, not the noise. The psalmist declared, "Even though I walk through the valley of the shadow of death, I will fear no evil, for you are with me; your rod and your staff, they comfort me" (Ps 23:4 ESV). The sheep willingly follow the shepherd into the dark valley because they know the shepherd *is there* to protect them and guide them safely through. Perhaps God seems distant to you because He is simply saying, "Trust Me, follow Me, and learn from Me."

Conclusion

In Luke 11, the disciples had a good day: They approached Jesus with perhaps the wisest request they would ever bring to Him: *Lord, teach us to pray.* He gave them the model on how to pray— in what we commonly refer to as the "Lord's Prayer"—then He shared a story to teach them to be persistent in prayer.

> He also said to them: "Suppose one of you has a friend and goes to him at midnight and says to him, 'Friend, lend me three loaves of bread, because a friend of mine on a journey has come to me, and I don't have anything to offer him.' Then he will answer from inside and say, 'Don't bother me! The door is already locked, and my children and I have gone to bed. I can't get up to give you anything.' I tell you, even though he won't get up and give him anything because he is his friend, yet because of his friend's persistence, he will get up and give him as much as he needs." (Luke 11:5–8)

This Scripture is not teaching us that nagging God is the key to getting our prayers answered. It teaches us that if we are willing to help a friend in the time of need, God is more than willing to help us when we come to Him with our concerns. Jesus then told His disciples to be persistent in prayer: "So I say to you, keep asking, and it will be given to you. Keep searching, and you will find. Keep knocking, and the door will be opened to you. For everyone who asks receives, and the one who searches finds, and to the one who knocks, the door will be opened" (Luke 11:9–10). Notice the verbs prominently placed in this text: *ask*, *seek*, and *knock*. Notice the promised results of fervent prayer found in verse 10: *receive*, *find*, and the phrase, *"the door will be opened."* If God seems distant to you, do not give up. Do not be discouraged. Keep your face turned toward heaven and be persistent in your prayers, and in due season God will reward your faith.

Endnotes

1. Henry Blackaby, Richard Blackaby, Claude King, *Experiencing God: Knowing and Doing the Will of God*, revised and expanded (Nashville: B&H Publishing, 2008), 45.

2. Max Lucado, *God Came Near* (Nashville: Thomas Nelson, 2004).

3. William McDonald, "Hebrews," in *Believer's Bible Commentary*, ed. Arthur Farstad (Nashville: Thomas Nelson, 1995), E-Sword Electronic Edition.

4. Ravi Zacharias, *Has Christianity Failed You?* (Grand Rapids: Zondervan, 2010), 157.

5. Charles H. Spurgeon, *The Treasury of David*, http://www.spurgeon.org/treasury/ps130.htm, accessed December 15, 2012.

CONCLUSION

While this book was in the final stages of being written, heartbreak gripped America as shootings took the lives of more than two dozen adults and children at a Connecticut elementary school. With twenty-eight victims killed, December 14, 2012 would witness the second deadliest school shooting in United States history. Only the 2007 massacre at Virginia Tech would claim more lives (32).

Reverend Will Marotti was among those called by authorities to assist in the immediate aftermath of the crime. Marotti, a graduate of Liberty University, planted New Life Church in his native Connecticut in the late 1990s. Now a well-known and respected clergyman in the region, Marotti was committed to minister to the victims in Newtown in any way possible. Shortly after the news broke of the killings, Marotti's phone rang, and he was summoned to help.

"The immensity of this tragedy and the carnage at the crime scene was beyond description," he said. "Officers with decades of service in law enforcement—women and men who had, as they say, 'seen it all'—were openly weeping." During that first day of the tragedy, officers, paramedics, clergy, and other first-responders worked until early morning hours.

In what Marotti described as "the most painful day of my entire ministry," he was among the chaplains sent to deliver news of the deaths to some of the families. As Reverend Marotti, a mental health professional, and a Connecticut State Trooper entered one of the first homes notified, the family members looked at the trio of responders with anxious expressions. "The family members looked at us as if they were pleading to hear good news," said Marotti. "But they seemed to know the terrible report that they were about to hear."

As an awkward moment of silence filled the room, the state trooper requested something of the pastor that is not heard every day from a law enforcement officer: "Reverend, would you please say a prayer?"

Looking back on those days, Marotti observed: "Connecticut is not known as a bastion of fervent Christianity. But there was much, much prayer going on that day. But it was just natural to pray—just obvious. When tragedy comes along, what can you do but *pray*?"

Prayer: Some Final Facts and Application

Throughout this book we have addressed questions about prayer, unpacking many of the related theological and philosophical implications. In closing we will take note of a few additional realities about prayer and do our best to consider how these apply to our lives. This is important for all of us because, from a biblical perspective, prayer is not merely *theoretical*. True prayer, life-changing prayer is about the *personal* and the *actual*. It is fine to study prayer; it is better still to *live it*.

The Universality of Prayer

Prayer is ubiquitous. People everywhere pray. I (Alex) think the universality of prayer is a potent argument for God's existence. Prayer is not just common among all peoples; it is *inherent*. Prayer is not merely a phenomenon of religious cultures; all cultures are religious.

While I was sharing the gospel with a man from Greece (who explained to me that he was not religious), he said, "I don't know anyone, anywhere who does not at some point in their life, just, um . . ." At that point the man held his arms open wide, palms facing up, and looked up to the sky with a helpless expression on his face. Studying his gesture, I asked, "What do you mean?" In broken English he poignantly said, "Sooner or later, we all must say to God, 'Have mercy on me. Help me. I need You.'"

Indeed. Though the words and postures vary, the ubiquity of prayer cannot be missed. Prayer to God—whom we seem intuitively to know can hear—is universal.

The Necessity of Prayer

Prayer is, it appears, a necessity. Before a debate with a certain atheist, I asked if he had ever prayed. "Once," he answered. "When our baby daughter was very sick." Similar sentiments I have heard from others indicate that some see prayer as a type of moral responsibility. In that sense prayer is seen as somehow necessary.

But prayer also seems to be an *emotional* necessity. We may not always pray as we should, but when asked about the subject, most people *want* to pray at times and indicate that they are glad they can.

While interviewing individuals for our previous book *10 Questions Every Christian Must Answer*,[1] I spoke with more than a dozen atheists and skeptics who (privately) admitted to me that they occasionally prayed. It seems prayer is something all individuals, sooner or later, feel compelled to do.

Author Bruce Sheiman concurs, though I realize that many of his fellow atheists would (at least publicly) disagree. Sheiman convincingly argues that prayer and the desire to connect with something beyond ourselves is essentially *unavoidable*:

> Most atheists will say they can do without the "infinite," but I assert that this is the core of what it means to be human and by extension, religious. In essence, I am saying that we are, even the atheists among us, *homo religious*. It's just that atheists cannot believe in God. (But) scratch the

surface and you will find that all atheists want to believe in some form of the Absolute.[2]

In an interview dealing with the subject of recovery and emotional stability after a trauma, professor of psychology Jeffrey Sweatt said, "In cases of severe emotional stress, counseling is important. Counseling can help, of course, but prayer and spiritual healing are necessities."[3]

The Accessibility of Prayer

The story is told of three preachers who were sitting in a church discussing what was the most appropriate and efficacious position to assume when praying. A telephone repairman was in the background overhearing the conversation. One minister said that the most important things were clasped hands and a bowed head. Another said that kneeling was essential to vibrant prayer. The third minister present said that humbly lying face down, prostrate on the floor was the key to more powerful prayer. Listening to this, the telephone repairman spoke up and said, "The most powerful praying I ever did was as I dangled upside down, hanging from a telephone pole high above the ground!"

What a blessing it is that all people—*all people*—can pray. The height one's prayer may reach is not contingent on how much money one has or one's standing within social circles; neither does prayer depend on any of the things we humans commonly deem important. God measures our hearts, not our wealth or perceived importance. He cares more about our sincerity than our substance! God does not show partiality (Acts 10:34; Jas 2:1). No matter his or her background, each person may have as strong a prayer life as they are willing to pursue.

The Benefits of Prayer

Even some atheists admit that not only is prayer universally practiced by people of all cultures; prayer is actually beneficial.

In his book *An Atheist Defends Religion*, Bruce Sheiman documents that prayer is beneficial whether or not one believes in an omniscient God who is listening and who answers. Citing control-group studies conducted at Harvard, Duke, and the University of Virginia, Sheiman agrees that prayer contributes to, "reduced stress, lowered blood pressure, diminished anxiety, and augmented immune response."[4]

The Privilege of Prayer

A famous restaurant chain promises that at their eating establishment "You're family." But when I eat with relatives, I do not have to pay. And as much as the "you're family" motif is touted, if the meal is unsatisfactory, I cannot sit with the owner and discuss it. The ballyhoo about being in the family is more style than substance. But what an honor it is to be able to get hold of the God of the universe! I cannot call the White House and speak with the president. But as a Christian, I can bow my head, open my heart, and pray knowing that God will hear. Hebrews 4:16 encourages us to come before God "boldly." Some translations use the word "confidently" or even, "fearlessly." Christians enjoy privilege beyond measure in knowing that they may call on God at any time. "Prayer is like a child's communion with a father. Because the Christian is one who has been born into the family of God, it is as natural to pray as it is for an earthly child to ask his or her father for the things he or she needs."[5]

Adoniram Judson was a great missionary to Asian countries in the early 1800s. Stories of God's work through Judson have become missionary lore that has inspired generations. Speaking of the privilege of praying to God for provisions, Judson said, "I never prayed sincerely and earnestly for anything but it came at some time; no matter at how distant a day, somehow, in some shape, probably the least I would have devised, it came."[6] God's answers may come in ways that surprise us (they usually do), but to be able to bring our needs to Him is indeed an honor.

The Promises of Prayer

The greatest leaders throughout church history have—not coincidentally—pursued the most robust prayer lives. Great spiritual leaders understand that God's Word is our sourcebook for understanding more about prayer. Martin Luther studied the Bible at length to find out all that it said about prayer, confidently appropriating what he found. Luther would pray for three hours each day, "bluntly holding out God's promises (to Him), and demanding that He keep them."[7]

I (Alex) have always been intrigued by Jer 33:3, in which God offers, "Call to Me and I will answer you and tell you great and incomprehensible things you do not know." There are many such promises in Scripture regarding the myriad of things God does in response to the prayers of His people.

- **God promises to hear and to act:** "Now this is the confidence we have before Him: Whenever we ask anything according to His will, He hears us. And if we know that He hears whatever we ask, we know that we have what we have asked Him for" (1 John 5:14–15).

- **God promises that prayer gets even more powerful when Christians intercede together with unified hearts and minds:** "If two of you on earth agree about any matter that you pray for, it will be done for you by My Father in heaven. For where two or three are gathered together in My name, I am there among them" (Matt 18:19–20).

- **God makes near-unconditional promises to the church regarding prayer in John 16:23:** "I assure you: Anything you ask the Father in My name, He will give you."

- **God promises that prayer to Him will yield tangible results:** "Keep asking, and it will be given to you. Keep searching, and you will find. Keep knocking, and the door will be opened to you. For everyone who asks receives, and the one who searches finds, and to the one who knocks, the door will be opened" (Matt 7:7–8; Luke 11:9–10).

- **Beyond our material needs, God promises emotional blessings that come about through prayer:** "Don't worry about anything, but in everything, through prayer and petition with thanksgiving, let your requests be made known to God. And the peace of God, which surpasses every thought, will guard your hearts and minds in Christ Jesus" (Phil 4:6–7; see also Isa 26:3).

The Mystery of Prayer

As clear as the Bible makes it, much is still mysterious and unknown about prayer. How does God hear the prayers of billions of people all at once? How does God act in the life of one individual while at the same time managing the innumerable other contingencies of the universe that might possibly be affected? Do our prayers change God's plans? Do they ultimately cause changes in circumstances? Does prayer primarily change us?

C. S. Lewis described the misconceptions he held about prayer before becoming a Christian. Perhaps as many do prior to conversion, Lewis assumed that prayer was more about achieving mere "states of mind," rather than communing with a personal God who responds in tangible ways.[8] Lewis rightly came to understand that true prayer involves an objective *relationship* (with God) and not just a subjective *feeling* (within oneself).

One might wonder why God created prayer at all. He could have simply wound up the universe like a toy, programming from the beginning all circumstances and outcomes. Some think that is how things really are, but I disagree. In such a deterministic universe, prayer would not be needed. Yet prayer exists. Why? Because God gives humans the opportunity to enter into a relationship with Him.

A Christian's prayer life may include times of confident assurance, feelings of wonder, and admissions of ignorance. There is mystery in prayer because there is mystery in God.

The Mandate of Prayer

God's Word commands His people to pray. First Thessalonians 5:17 says, "Pray constantly." Philippians 4:6 says, "In everything through prayer and petition . . . , let your requests be made known to God." In 1 Tim 2:8, Paul wrote, "I want the men in every place to pray, lifting up holy hands without anger or argument."

God's people are to be a people of prayer, but not of perfunctory, grudging, obligatory prayer. They are to be a people who know their God and who communicate with Him intimately. Prayer is also expected by believers for other believers. Notice in Eph 6:18 that the reality of prayer in a Christian's life is *understood:* "Pray at all times in the Spirit with every prayer and request, and stay alert in this with all perseverance and intercession for all the saints."

Jesus said, "When you pray, go into your private room, shut your door, and pray to your Father who is in secret" (Matt 6:6). Jesus' instructions on *how* to pray presuppose that people *will* pray. For the Christian the pursuit of a robust prayer life is not a mere suggestion or an option. It is commanded and for our own good.

And So We Pray

It is often said that prayer is the nerve that moves the muscle of God. That being the case, may Christ move His body to touch that nerve with greater impact than ever before. To that end each one of us may play a role.

Endnotes

1. Alex McFarland and Elmer Towns, *10 Questions Every Christian Must Answer* (Nashville: B&H Academic, 2011).

2. Bruce Sheiman, *An Atheist Defends Religion* (New York: Penguin/ Alpha Books, 2009), 50.

3. "Exploring the Word," www.afr.net, accessed December 18, 2012.

4. Sheiman, *An Atheist Defends Religion*, 79–80.

5. Billy Graham and Charles G. Ward, eds., *The Billy Graham Christian Worker's Handbook* (Minneapolis: World Wide Publications, 1996), 234.

6. Quoted in E. M. Bounds, *Purpose in Prayer*, Christian Classics Ethereal Library, http://www.ccel.org/ccel/bounds/purpose.VI.html, accessed September 16, 2013.

7. Michael Reeves, *The Unquenchable Flame: Discovering the Heart of the Reformation* (Nashville: B&H Academic, 2009), 59.

8. C. S. Lewis, *Surprised by Joy* (New York: Harcourt, Brace, and Jovanovich, 1984), 168.

Subject Index